Encouraging Conversation

Resources for Talking about Same-Sex Blessings

Encouraging Conversation

Resources for Talking about Same-Sex Blessings

Edited by Fredrica Harris Thompsett

Foreword by V. Gene Robinson

Morehouse Publishing
NEW YORK · HARRISBURG · DENVER

Center for the Ministry of Teaching
Virginia Theological Seminary
Alexandria, VA 22304

Morehouse Publishing, 4775 Linglestown Road, Harrisburg, PA 17112

Morehouse Publishing, 445 Fifth Avenue, New York, NY 10016

Morehouse Publishing is an imprint of Church Publishing Incorporated.
www.churchpublishing.org

Cover design by Laurie Klein Westhafer
Typeset by Rose Design

Library of Congress Cataloging-in-Publication Data

A catalog record of this book is available from the Library of Congress.

ISBN-13: 978-0-8192-2873-4 (pbk.)
ISBN-13: 978-0-8192-2874-1 (ebook)

Printed in the United States of America

CONTENTS

FOREWORD

"Sex is dirty; save it for the one you love!" If you are a baby boomer, this is probably the double-edged (and crazy-making) message you got from your parents. In the 1970s, early gay activists were preaching "Gay is good!" while fundamentalists were doubling down on "You are an abomination!" In the 1980s, in the midst of the AIDS crisis, sex became associated with death in a way that cast a cloud over sexuality—both gay and straight. In the new millennium, thirty-two states (as of this writing) constitutionally ban gay marriage, while in nine states and the District of Columbia, same-sex couples are legally free to marry. Is it any wonder we are confused about sexuality?

People of faith are right in the middle of this cultural shift toward the acceptance of gay, lesbian, bisexual, and transgender people. Sometimes they reassert a traditional and blanket condemnation of anything outside heterosexuality. Sometimes they go where they have never gone before to welcome gay, lesbian, bisexual, and transgender people and affirm their relationships—and do so in the name of the God they believe in. Let's face it: The number one enemy of the full acceptance of LGBT people and their faithful relationships is still too often religion. Even non-religious people use religious arguments against us. No wonder it is confusing when a church recommends liturgical resources for blessing same-sex couples.

Pervasive among religious people is a resistance to having meaningful, honest, and personal conversation about this important reality of what it means to be human. Part of that resistance, I suspect, is a genuine shyness and vulnerability. "How can I have this conversation without revealing what I think, feel, and do sexually? And that is my personal business, and no one else's." But for gay, lesbian, bisexual, and transgender people, it is *not* merely personal, since what is at stake is our legal and constitutional right to live our authentic lives and to have our relationships supported and protected by the civil government, as do our heterosexual counterparts.

So why is it so hard to talk about this? What scares us so much? It has always amazed me that Christians shy away from difference of opinion and the conflict that often results. Jesus' entire ministry was fraught with conflict, as he challenged and changed the tradition in which he was reared. The early church was filled with controversy and conflict. St. Paul didn't write all those epistles to fledgling churches around the Mediterranean to praise them for the great job they were doing; he wrote to guide them through the conflict they were experiencing. Conflict is in the church's DNA! Yet we cower in the face of conflict and difference of opinion as if it threatens us with death. Sometimes the death of a former understanding in favor of a new understanding can feel like real death, but thoughtful people of faith must learn to tell the difference between the two and embrace the hard conversations we need to have.

Most heterosexual people, especially religious ones, will tell you they are sick and tired of talking about sexuality all the time. At its best, such a sentiment might reflect a desire not to focus on the issues of homosexuality that have diverted us from our larger mission as a church. But I suspect that part of that sentiment is more like a resistance to broadening the conversation about the sex lives of gay people into a thorough discussion of *human* sexuality and its meaning for all of us.

Heterosexuals may be tired of talking about gay sex, but they can't be tired of talking about human sexuality because that discussion has hardly begun! We began the sexuality discussion as the "gay" and "straight" communities. Then lesbians spoke up and said, "You know, our experience as lesbians is different from that of gay men." And so we became "straight" and "gay and lesbian." Then bisexual and transgender people came forward to point out that their experience was more different still. And we became "straight" and "LGBT." Further refinement of our sexual identities continues with new letters being added all the time: "Q" for questioning, and/ or queer; "I" for intersex. Who knows how many letters we'll be adding as the diversity among us is explored? And yet, there sits "straight" as one big blob of heterosexuality, as if no diversity exists among straight people!

I often encourage straight audiences to go "talk amongst your-selves" about your *own* sexuality and the vast diversity that exists within the "straight community." "What letters would you use to describe *your* diversity?" I ask them. They usually laugh—nervously, I might add—because heterosexual people have not done the work, and they know it! While LGBT people have had to stay up late into the night learning to put words around their thoughts, feelings, and experiences in order to survive in a heterocentric world, heterosexual people can skate along on the heteronormative ice provided for them by the culture. Now it's time for straight people to get to work! And would it be too much to suggest that they might benefit from the work the LGBT community has been doing? I think not.

There has been no push for heterosexuals to have those conversations, and besides, they are hard, and they may make us feel exposed and vulnerable. But as the LGBT community has shown, these conversations can be liberating and affirming. For religious LGBT people, these conversations have led to a deeper, more expansive understanding of God's goodness and grace—an understanding that has far-reaching ramifications for all of life. I want heterosexual people to experience that deeper understanding of God and God's love for all of us. That won't happen unless we have the hard conversations.

It's time for the discussions of homosexuality to expand into real, honest, and vulnerable conversations about what it means to be human, what it means to be an embodied, physical being, and what God wants for us. It's time for straight people to talk *with* gay people, not just *about* us. It's time to explore what transgender people have to teach all of us, gay and straight alike, about gender fluidity and sexual identity—parts of all of us we seldom acknowledge. And it's time we actually *believe* that God has a fanciful and dramatic flair for diversity, and "it is good." It could even be that we are moving toward acknowledging that each of us has our own unique set of experiences that have formed us as sexual beings. Now that's an encouraging conversation worth having! And I think God would be very pleased.

V. Gene Robinson

INTRODUCTION

When I was young, the family dining room table was a provocative locus for conversation. I wonder if families today find this to be true? I was fortunate to grow up with the opportunity to discuss almost anything with my parents . . . that is, anything except sexuality. We regularly talked about politics, the supposed "evils" of labor unions (my attorney father worked for Henry Ford), and even my great-grandfather's drinking. My lively parents were far from prudish, yet mention of sexuality, let alone homosexuality, was seemingly forbidden.

Times have changed. Private as well as public conversations about sexuality, including homosexuality, are a regular component of North American culture. This pattern, however, does not mean that most of us are either equipped or eager to address such complex issues, even within our own family circles. When these conversations move into religious communities and denominations, rancorous public debate has often ensued. Looking for better ways to begin the dialogue, this collection of resources is designed to encourage and support thoughtful conversation about homosexuality.

For decades, there have been conversations in churches about sexuality that have been thoughtful and inspiring, as well as troubling and divisive. The compelling story of these events and debates over the past fifty years in the Episcopal Church and wider Anglican

Communion has recently been published.[1] Since the 1979 General Convention's open hearing on human sexuality, I have been engaged in these discussions. I remain personally committed to opening up conversations in which our faithfulness as people of God allows us to respond attentively to our lesbian, gay, bisexual, and transgendered (LGBT) sisters and brothers.

As a denomination shaped by prayer and thanksgiving, members of the Episcopal Church are now requested to consider a new opportunity for extending God's blessings. The specific focus is the Episcopal Church's recent decision at the 2012 General Convention to authorize a liturgical rite for blessing same-sex unions. The rite itself, called "The Witnessing and Blessing of a Lifelong Covenant," is both provisional and optional. Its provisional use indicates that, as is the case with any significant liturgical change, it will be monitored and considered again at the 2015 General Convention. This new rite is not mandatory, and its use must receive the local bishop's permission. Congregations and dioceses, however, are specifically invited to initiate discussion, if they have not already, about the theology and practice of blessing same-sex unions. Wide-ranging theological reports and other study resources and guidelines are available, as is the extensive report of the 2012 Standing Commission on Liturgy and Music: *I Will Bless You and You Will Be a Blessing.*[2]

Encouraging Conversation is unique in that it prompts individuals, vestries, and parishes to consider joining the conversation with stories from the past decade. *Encouraging Conversation* offers a short collection of sermons, guidelines, processes, stories, and reflections

---

1. Caroline J. Addington Hall, *A Thorn in the Flesh: How Gay Sexuality Is Changing the Episcopal Church* (Rowman & Littlefield, 2013).

2. Standing Commission on Liturgy and Music, *Liturgical Resources I: I Will Bless You and You Will Be a Blessing* (Church Publishing, 2013).

on "how we did it in our parish." It is intended for those who are just beginning to wade into these conversational waters, as well as for those who are looking for positive approaches toward same-sex blessings. Authors speak from their local context, and a variety of cultural and ethnic perspectives is offered. Contributors include clergy, lay leaders, Episcopalians both young and old, theologians, preachers, authors, diocesan representatives, and liturgists.

How to begin? I invite you to bring your own questions as you peruse these chapters. Is there a contribution in this volume that you would like to share, to discuss with another? What insights, what images, what story from your own experience might you consider sharing with others? What supportive opportunities would help you, and others you know, faithfully enter the conversation?

I also wish to persuade you to bring with you a sense of thanksgiving. Thanksgiving for a Church that seeks to address controversy faithfully.[3] Thanksgiving for local faith communities that nourish and challenge us. Thanksgiving for the testimonies, struggles, scholarship, legacies, and labor of LBGT Christians and their allies.

As these conversations come to life and deepen, I am particularly thankful for colleagues and friends who contributed their words and wisdom to this volume, including Nancy Bryan of Church Publishing, Inc. Each of you, in your own unique way, encourages faithful conversation.

Fredrica Harris Thompsett
Cape Cod and Cambridge, Massachusetts

---

3. Our biblical, Anglican, and Episcopal ancestors have a long history of addressing disagreements with varied success. For a short overview of some of these controversies, see my volume to the New Church's Teaching Series, Fredrica Harris Thompsett, *Living with History* (Cowley Publications, 1999).

CHAPTER 1

Our Congregational Process of Conversation about Same-Sex Blessings[1]

Lowell Grisham

Our Story

In the fall of 2002, a retired priest who served as an associate in our parish said in a sermon that he wished our congregation would honor the commitments of our gay couples who are in life-long loving relationships. He wished we could offer those couples the church's pastoral blessing, to let them experience the support that he and his wife of forty-three years had enjoyed. His words created a buzz.

(A note about our parish: In 2002 Fayetteville was a town of around sixty thousand people. It is a college town, and so it tends to be a bit more progressive than some other Arkansas communities. We are culturally influenced by the South with some Midwestern and Western flavors.)

---

1. The Reverend Lowell Grisham, rector of St. Paul's Episcopal Church, Fayetteville, Arkansas, and a member of the 2012 Standing Commission on Liturgy and Music, shared the story of this process prepared and written by members of the parish.

Early in 2003 we conducted a parish survey to ask the congregation whether or not we should engage in a conversation about the possibility of offering same-sex blessings. A high percentage of the congregation responded to the question. The results were mixed: 50 percent said "strongly agree" and another 15 percent said they "somewhat agree" that we were ready to begin such a conversation. It was obvious that there was a lot of energy in favor of engaging the issue. But a very significant minority of almost 22 percent said they "strongly disagree" with any proposal to initiate any conversation that might lead to our consideration of same-sex blessings.

Our vestry decided to honor the voice of that minority, choosing to delay any formal process of discernment. The vestry asked the clergy to produce some information to help the congregation better understand the theological, ecclesiological, and biblical issues. They asked for an informal process of education and reflection.

Through the monthly newsletter, we published brief articles from a wide range of perspectives. We traced the church's General Convention resolutions about human sexuality. We offered theological and biblical resources from pro and con positions, including material from the American Anglican Council. Since the rector was for blessings, he consulted with his friend the Reverend Kendall Harmon of South Carolina to recommend the best resources we could use to present the argument against blessings. Our curate, a former medical school faculty member, wrote an essay and offered a class about human sexuality from a scientific point of view. Each of our clergy preached on the topic at some point. One of the interesting resources we used was a biblical study of homosexuality written by a Southern Baptist minister, *A Letter to Louise*.[2]

Prior to attending the General Convention in the summer of 2003, the rector preached a sermon articulating his thoughts about the inclusion of gay and lesbian members in the life of the church.

Our parish followed the events of the 2003 General Convention, during which Gene Robinson was confirmed as the Episcopal Church's first gay bishop in a publicly open relationship. The 2003 General Convention acknowledged that "we recognize that local faith communities are operating within the bounds of our common life as they explore and experience liturgies celebrating and blessing same-sex unions." The convention also reaffirmed the 1999 resolution calling the church to "continued prayer, study, and discernment on the pastoral care for gay and lesbian persons, to facilitate as wide a conversation of discernment as possible throughout the church."

After the 2003 General Convention, we offered several venues for study and conversation. Among the most helpful things we did was to recruit a group of parishioners to participate in a reconciliation process written by Bishop Steven Charleston called *Good News: A Congregational Resource for Reconciliation*. We recruited a balanced number of parishioners with strong feelings about same-gender blessings from both sides of the debate. We asked them to go through the *Good News* series of structured conversations focusing on the themes of justice, compassion, and reconciliation. At the end of the four sessions, the participants responded enthusiastically about their experience. As one participant said, "No one's mind was changed, but I left loving every one of those people in that room."

---

2. Bruce Lowe, *A Letter to Louise: A Biblical Affirmation of Homosexuality*, written in 2002, is available online at *http://godmademegay.blogspot.com/*.

The group recommended that the vestry go through the *Good News* process. We asked members of the first group to facilitate the vestry's engaging of the *Good News* resource by Bishop Steven Charleston. The exercise gave the vestry a set of skills for listening with deep respect. They learned how to seek reconciliation within disagreement.

Dean Scott Richardson of St. Paul's Cathedral, San Diego, came at the invitation of our McMichael Lecture series to speak on the topic "How Can We Live Together When We Believe Different Things?," reflecting on the New Testament church and on his own experience of serving in conflicted contexts.

In early 2005, the rector gave a two-fold charge to the vestry. First, he asked them to decide whether or not St. Paul's was ready to engage in a process of discernment that would lead to a decision about our position on same-gender blessings. If the answer was "no," that would end our consideration of any change, at least during his tenure as rector. If the answer was "yes," then he would ask the vestry to design a procedure to lead the whole congregation into a corporate discernment process. At the end of that congregational process, the vestry would come to a decision about our congregation's position on same-sex blessings. The rector said that the vestry could work through these two questions without any presumed time constraints. Let it take as long as it takes. He also asked that both decisions from the vestry be made by consensus.

The vestry made the question public and asked for input from the congregation. In their announcement, they reminded the congregation of our church's values for those living in intimate relationships: *"fidelity, monogamy, mutual affection and respect, careful, honest communication and the holy love which enables those in such relationships to see in each other the image of God"—2000 General Convention reso-lution D039. The Episcopal Church holds all its members accountable to those values in their life-long committed relationships. Further, the church denounces "promiscuity, exploitation and abusiveness in the relationships of any of our members."*

Then the vestry asked the congregation, "Are we ready to discuss whether or not to offer same-sex blessings?" We published the email addresses and telephone numbers of the vestry members.

The vestry set up alternating meetings to hear from both per-spectives. One month, the vestry listened to the views of those who supported blessings. The vestry gave ample time for everyone who came to express themselves. There was no debate, just clarifying questions to make sure that the vestry understood the perspective of all who spoke. The following month the vestry followed the same procedure, listening to those who opposed blessings. We were very clear in expressing our conviction that everyone would be heard, respected, and valued. We recognized that this *was* an issue on which very good people disagree. We vowed to hear one another, agree to disagree when we must, and remain in communion with each other in a spirit of compassion and respect.

Congregational input was energetic. The vestry e-mail inbox was active. After three months of listening, the vestry was ready to talk among themselves and decide. Their decision was clear: St. Paul's was ready for a discernment process. What more information do we need? What process shall we follow?

The vestry asked that the bishop come and help clarify how our conversation related to the wider Episcopal Church and the Angli-can Communion. To help educate everyone further, we created an information table with resources including *To Set Our Hope on*

Christ, the Episcopal Church's response to the Windsor Report, and used as our Lenten study book, *For Fidelity* by Catherine Wallace, a strong defense of sexual fidelity. Diverse resources were noted as well: In opposition to blessings were "Without Form and Void," an article by Kendall Harmon, and *True Union in the Body?* by Archbishop Drexel Gomez; and in favor of blessings was *This Far by Grace* by Bishop Neil Alexander.

The vestry decided that the heart of the congregational process would be four parish meetings following the *Good News* model for reconciliation. Vestry members would sit at small tables to listen and facilitate conversation. Since we had more participants than we had vestry to facilitate, we recruited several people with group process skills to help guide other tables and to report the conversational content back to the vestry.

The *Good News* process allows for each person to have a voice and to be heard without being argued with or responded to. It places a high value upon listening and upon participants being self-defined. It creates an atmosphere of community and respect. Nearly all of the evaluations that we received from those who participated were very positive. People felt free to express their honest views in a context of respect and reconciliation. At the final session, the bishop came to address questions about the implications for the wider church. When the four parish meetings were over, the vestry had heard the parish, and parishioners had listened to one another.

When the vestry convened to reflect on what they had learned, there was a great deal of awe and appreciation for what the community had been through. It felt like a holy experience. As the members of the vestry expressed their own hearts, each speaking one at a time, without debate or argument, every member expressed a belief that offering a pastoral rite of blessing for our committed gay couples was the right thing to do. Each member expressed care and concern for those who would disagree with them. After we had listened to one another, there was a clear consensus.

The final wording of the resolution passed by the vestry in September, 2005 was as follows: *The Vestry of St. Paul's Episcopal Church expresses its support for our church's offering of a rite of blessing as a resource for pastoral care for our gay and lesbian members who wish to make a lifelong, loving commitment of mutual fidelity as a couple. By this resolution we communicate our position to our clergy, our Bishop and the upcoming General Convention of the Episcopal Church.*

The announcement to the parish includes some further elaboration, explaining that we would honor the House of Bishop's moratorium, so there would be no blessings performed until after the 2006 General Convention, and only if offering a pastoral rite of blessing would conform to the decisions of the General Convention. Since the vestry saw this resolution as part of their contribution to the whole church's discussion of pastoral care for all our members, they mailed a copy of it to each bishop and e-mailed it to the House of Deputies.

In their communication with the parish, the vestry expressed particular concern for our parishioners who would find this decision disappointing and painful. The vestry reaffirmed its intention to continue the spirit of our parish conversations to promote our willingness to honor one another in our disagreements and to remain in communion with each other, seeking reconciliation through Christ's peace which transcends all our divisions.

Around a half-dozen families or individuals who felt the decision was not one that they could consent to and remain in the parish chose to leave. Earlier in the process, a few others left us. Somewhere between 2 percent and 3 percent of our members left during the entire process and conversation. Some, but not all, of those families have now returned to St. Paul's. The Every Member Canvass that we undertook a few months later was a strong one, resulting in pledges that were 15 percent above the previous year's giving. Attendance continued to grow, as did membership.

Shortly after the General Convention of 2006, our bishop, Larry Maze, told St. Paul's that there was nothing decided at the convention that would prevent our congregation from acting on what we had discerned. He gave us permission to offer rites of pastoral blessing for our committed same-sex couples. We followed a process of preparation for union that was similar to what we used for pre-marital preparation, and we performed our first series of blessings. They were worship services of deep joy and love.

Not long after our new bishop, Larry Benfield, was ordained, he asked that Arkansas congregations offering same-sex blessings refrain from certain liturgical actions in order to distinguish the blessings from the sacrament of marriage—vows, exchange of rings, and joining of hands. We modified our service to conform to the bishop's instruction.

Since those days our attendance, program, and stewardship have continued to grow. This year our discernment process has been about our need to expand our worship space because we find the church is full for two services on many Sundays. We are also discussing our need for more space in all areas of our ministry. We anticipate the possibility that we will launch a capital drive to underwrite a major expansion of both worship and program facilities in the foreseeable future.

An Outline of Our Process

2003—The congregation completed a survey.

We found a majority was willing to engage a conversation about the possibility of offering blessings to our members who were in committed same-gender loving relationships; but almost 22 percent said they strongly disagreed with initiating such a conversation. Out of respect for that minority, we postponed a process and engaged in a period of education and information.

2003–2004—Educational offerings from various theological perspectives were presented.

Late 2003—A small group engaged the *Good News* reconciliation process.

Participants were evenly divided, for and against blessings. Minds weren't changed, but people listened with respect and affection. The group recommended that the vestry experience the Good News process.

2004—The vestry engaged in the *Good News* reconciliation process.

2005—The rector charged the vestry to decide whether or not to lead the congregation in engaging in a process of conversation about same-sex blessings.

After hearing from parishioners from all sides of the issues, the vestry decided to lead a congregational discernment process.

2005—The congregation engaged in conversation.

We supplied resources from a variety of positions.

The congregation participated in four parish meetings following the Good News model.

September 2005—A vestry consensus endorsed offering of a rite of blessing.

Respecting the House of Bishop's moratorium, we postponed any blessing until after the 2006 General Convention. We communicated the text of our resolution to the House of Bishops and House of Deputies in anticipation of the 2006 General Convention.

2006—After the General Convention, the bishop gave St. Paul's permission to act on what we had discerned. In October, 2006 we celebrated our first rites of union for same-sex couples.

❖ ❖ ❖

Lowell Grisham is the Rector of St. Paul's Episcopal Church in Fayetteville, Arkansas. A native of Mississippi, he is married and his two children are now bringing grandchildren into the world, to his great delight.

CHAPTER 2

A Civil Union Homily[1]

Martin L. Smith

Part of the fun of weddings and holy unions is meeting the other guests and relatives, and finding a lot out about the couple from the reception and the arrangements and the service. A couple tell us a lot about themselves and we are all going to be delighted and intrigued over this weekend of celebration. We can discover a whole lot if we are all eyes and ears, and it has already started in the service with the gospel passage that Thomas and Tom have chosen to put as a hallmark on their relationship.

John the Baptist is trying to run his reform movement from jail and time is running out. He needs to know whether Jesus is the One who is to come, or should they keep on looking for someone else. Jesus doesn't give a straight answer. He just points to the evidence that people are being set free from what blights and stunts life and thwarts its fullness. "The blind receive their sight, the lame walk, the lepers are cleansed, the deaf hear, the dead are raised, and the poor have good news brought to them" (Matthew 11:5).

---

1. This sermon was preached at the blessing of the union of Thomas James Brown and Thomas Nordboe Mousin, June 28, 2003. It is included in a resource from the Episcopal Diocese of Vermont, *Intimate Human Relations: Resources for Conversation*, 2004, pp. 41–42.

Lots of anxious people are asking these days what authority we have to celebrate in church the union of a man with a man, and if we know the gospel, we don't have to give a straight answer, any more than Jesus did. We point to the evidence of grace abounding in the relationship and the blessings spreading all around from the relationship. And we just say "Blessed is anyone who takes no offense at us." The blessing of a gay relationship isn't a special concession to homosexuals, but one facet of the liberation itself that comes to us all through the good news. We just happen to be people who have had our eyes opened, our ears unstopped, and we can see and tell that the intimacy and commitment and the faithfulness and hospitality of two men in love in Christ are manifestations of the gospel liberation meant for all. It's wonderful but it isn't weird. It's just the good news taking hold—at long last.

There's bound to be a poignancy to this service precisely because blessing services are still new, and Thomas and Tom have the special vocation of pioneers. For millennia our gay and lesbian predecessors lived with the poverty of having their relationship invalidated and unrecognized, in the blindness of the closet, the lameness of secrecy, the leper's stigma of the rejected. Four thousand years is a long time to wait. But now the time has come for liberation to take hold, and it is doing so. And if anyone asks by what authority we perform this controversial blessing, we do have an answer even if it is not a very straight answer, but an answer with a queer ring.

When a wedding of a man and woman takes place in church, it takes place under the authority of immemorial tradition and precedent. From the dawn of humanity, men and women have been coupled to make a family, have children, and nurture the next generation. When the union of a man and a man takes place in church, there is no authority from the past. Instead, the blessing is taking place under the authority of the future.

"Are you the One who is to come?" That title, the One who is to come, is the greatest title for Jesus as the Christ. Jesus is the one who does not tie us to the past, but recruits us to join him in making God's future present in the here and the now. As soon as we recognize Jesus for who he truly is, we realize that God's future is too real to be postponed any longer. We can't think of it as an ideal realm that always stays over the horizon, at the other end of a rainbow that we can never actually reach. Jesus had the chutzpah to proclaim that the time of waiting is over—enough already!—and the reign of God has arrived. It is up to us to live as an outpost of the future in the present, insistent on acting as if God's blessed future is something we can enjoy today.

Well, I am sure that Tom and Thomas really did show their theology in the choice of the gospel. But the unconscious is a strange thing in the way it guides us. This question, "Are you the One who is to come, or are we to wait for another?" is almost word for word the question any man asks about his partner when he falls in love. "Is he the one I have been waiting for, or should I go on looking for someone else? Has the search ended, or is the one for me someone else, someone I haven't met yet?" Perhaps unconsciously our friends have shown us something of the vulnerability of commitment. There is so much risk in deciding not to go on looking, not to carry on waiting, but to choose. He is the one, this is the moment I let go of searching and waiting. I choose the one who has found me and the one I have found, the one who is here and now.

Commitment is necessarily an act of faith. If I could guarantee that I would stay the same, if I could guarantee that my partner would stay the same, we could work out pretty well the odds of making it all work. But the very nature of love is the willingness to be changed by love, by the one we love, and by the experiment of union with the one we love. We don't know who we are turning into when we risk intimacy.

Now a few of you know how much the mystery of the Trinity means to me—it has been central in my life of faith and in my writings and preaching—and so Trinity Sunday is almost my favorite Sunday in the year. This year I celebrated it in a very special way. I went to a Unitarian Church. Needless to say there had to be a strong love interest to get me to do that on Trinity Sunday. Someone very dear to me was giving a testimony in the service. The service was full of blessings. And one of the most striking was a new hymn I had never sung before. In a superb call to give God many names, the hymn has a verse:

> Young, growing God, eager still to know,
>
> Willing to be changed by what you started.
>
> Quick to be delighted, singing as you go:
>
> Hail and hosanna! Young, growing God.

In just a few lines it brings to life the theology of the mystics— didn't Meister Eckhart proclaim that God is the *novissimus*, the newest of the new, the youngest of the young? And Brian Wren's hymn allows us to celebrate the great religious breakthrough of the twentieth century, the discovery of a God who is wedded to the evolutionary process of Creation, that God who is so vulnerably wedded to our unfolding through evolution and history that God is willing to be changed by what he started. A God who is not the immobile Ancient of Days defending immemorial custom and binding us to ancient law, but our intimate incarnate companion in a changing and emerging world embracing us, wedded to us, as we step together into what is unprecedented and new and risky and young.

For some people it is not only unbelievably scary, but outrageously blasphemous to claim that God didn't know what he was getting into when the big bang went off. But the Christian gospel really does claim that God got into it all the same. Jesus is the sign of God's sharing our embodiment. The Cross is the sign for all time that his willingness to be changed by what he started extends to sharing our suffering and death, the worst that can befall any and all of us, in order to make sure that we are held in life within his beating Heart, whatever happens.

So we turn to Thomas and Tom in blessing. They know what they are getting into, and yet they don't know really. Thomas and Tom are willing as men of faith to be changed by what they've started. What they do know is that their companion in what they've started is a living God, who is open to the new life they are making together, willing to suffer with them in their struggles, and to share in the joy and fruitfulness which is certain to flow in all sorts of ways from their union—some sure, some quite unpredictable. The One who is to come is here, and we don't have to wait for the wedding of God to us as we celebrate the wedding of heart to heart, body to body, and soul to soul of these excellent men and dearest of friends.

✛ ✛ ✛

The Reverend Martin L. Smith is a former member of the Society of St. John the Evangelist (SSJE). He is an author who has also served on the staff of the United States Holocaust Memorial Museum in Washington, D.C.

CHAPTER 3

The Process of Decision-Making Regarding Same-Sex Blessings

Mark Harris and Patricia Bird

Background

St. Peter's, Lewes, in the Diocese of Delaware, has been central to the community since 1681 and has reflected the conserving values of the area while being welcoming to all who wished to join the congregation. By the mid-1990s a substantial portion of the membership of St. Peter's was gay or lesbian and many of these members exercised leadership on all levels of church life.

In the early 1990s, under the direction of Bishop Cabell Tennis, a committee was formed to study the issue of blessing same-sex unions. This response team developed a diocesan-wide education and discussion format to discover ways of affirming homosexual persons as part of the faith community and to provide pastoral services to them.

The rector of St. Peter's, the Reverend Douglas Culton, a self-affirmed homosexual, was part of that committee. Bishop Tennis had allowed several clergy in the diocese to proceed with blessings in private contexts. During the late 1990s, Douglas Culton conducted several services of blessing of same-sex couples in private settings, but not in the church building itself. He had informed the bishop of these actions.

When the Reverend Wayne Wright was a candidate for election as bishop of Delaware, he was informed of the work being done and of the beginnings of a diocesan policy regarding such unions. He affirmed his willingness to see the process move forward, both during the search process and following his election in 1998.

On September 15, 2001, Bishop Wright issued *Standards to Guide a Common Practice for Services of Blessing*. These standards were reviewed by the Standing Committee and the Diocesan Council and were understood to be the product of the study, discussions, and actual services that had taken place over the previous six to eight years. The first of this set of standards concerned the congregational sanction of such services. It stated, "Blessing of same gender relationships, like other pastoral ministries, is a congregational ministry. The bishop is ready to support this ministry in congregations only where an educational process has been carried out and where there is substantial agreement among congregational leaders."

In November 2003 Douglas Culton resigned his position as Rector of St. Peter's for a position in New York City. The parish called the Reverend Patricia Bird as interim rector, and she began her work at St. Peter's in January 2004. The parish then began its process of calling a new rector.

When Patricia Bird arrived there were already several requests pending for same-sex blessings and, upon inquiry, she realized that St. Peter's had never undertaken an educational process or sought "substantial agreement among congregational leaders" as required by the Standards. Because there seemed to be a lack of agreement about where St. Peter's stood, she asked the couples in question to postpone their requests until the matter could be clarified or, if they were unwilling to wait, to seek an alternative setting for their blessing. By then there were a few parishes in the diocese that *had* completed the requirements of the Standards and she suggested that the couples contact these churches. She co-officiated at one such blessing held at St. Andrew's and St. Matthew's parish in Wilmington, Delaware, along with the Reverend Canon Lloyd Casson.

She and the staff, together with the vestry, believed that it was time for St. Peter's to undertake the educational process required by the diocese. She discussed this with Bishop Wright who felt that it would be beneficial for the parish to undertake the formal process of completing the requirements of the Standards.

The Challenge

The decision by the interim rector and the vestry to undertake the required educational process and parish discussions while the parish was also in the process of electing a new rector was the subject of considerable discussion in the spring of 2004. In the fall of 2003 and the spring of 2004 there were several short courses offered by clergy in the parish addressing biblical and theological concerns that the matter of blessings had raised. It was quickly realized that these were not focused and seemed biased. The vestry, at its March 2004 retreat, agreed to begin mapping out a more formal process for such discussions.

It became clear that (a) a letter to the parish introducing a specific and well-designed educational program needed to be put forward; (b) the memories of past leadership needed to be solicited so that whatever there was of an existing "customary" in the parish would be considered; and (c) this process needed to be concluded before any candidates for rector would be interviewed so that they would have the decision of the parish before them when they interviewed.

The November 2004 parish newsletter outlined the process that would be undertaken in the parish, addressing the question of whether or not to provide for the blessing of same-sex relationships at St. Peter's Church. The newsletter stated that "a subcommittee of the vestry is now designing an educational and conversational process that will encompass all points of view. This process will be presented to the vestry in November for its review and approval. All parishioners are urged to participate in the opportunities that will be presented. The process will follow "the Episcopal way" of incorporating scripture, tradition, and reason to arrive at an informed and responsible conclusion. In brief, scripture is the primary source of doctrine, reason involves the gifts of the Holy Spirit and our own ability to explore and comprehend God's word and to make responsible moral decisions, and tradition is the use of the wisdom of generations past to preserve essential truths. The vestry has definitively stated that no pre-determined outcome exists, and has set June 2005 as the target date for making a decision."

The Process

The Sub-Committee for the Process of Determining Policy Regarding Same-Gender Blessings at St. Peter's Church submitted its proposal to the vestry on November 9, 2004. It outlined a schedule of "conversations" for St. Peter's members to follow in educating ourselves regarding this decision in terms of scripture, Church tradition, and reason. At the conclusion of the process, the vestry, in consultation with the clergy, would decide whether St. Peter's would be able to offer same-sex blessings for its members. Systems were established to receive feedback from members of St. Peter's through these gatherings and by letters and e-mails, and by having members of the vestry available for individual conversations. Near the Day of Pentecost a special vestry meeting would be called to make this decision; the meeting would be preceded by opportunity for prayer.

Immediate Concerns Regarding the Announcement

The month leading up to the announcement of "the process" was accompanied by a heightened awareness of the challenge this process brought to parish life. Various concerns were expressed by parishioners, including those who thought the process was not necessary, one who feared St. Peter's would become "the Gay Church in Lewes," and another who felt the rector search should not be concurrent with the process.

The Educational Events

Following the report to the parish and the adoption of the process, the interim rector, on the advice of members of the Diocesan Committee on Human Sexuality (the committee first set up by Bishop Tennis), began to negotiate with a clergyperson from the diocese to be an outside facilitator at decision time, set for May 15, 2005.

The Right Reverend Paul Marshall, bishop of Bethlehem, Pennsylvania, and author of several articles and books on the subject of the church and homosexuality, opened the educational series on April 12, 2005 with a conversation about scripture. Some weeks later, Dr. Bruce Mullin, church historian on the faculty of the General Theological Seminary in New York, spoke to another gathering on the question of same-sex blessings in the context of church history and tradition. Between seventy and eighty people attended each session.

In late April of that year, several comments surfaced that both speakers were biased towards same-sex blessings. Could we find a voice equally studied and pastoral that more clearly represented views opposed to blessing same-sex unions? We were fortunate that the Reverend Charles Osburger of Wye Parish in the Diocese of Easton, Maryland, was able to make a presentation. He was well acquainted with the issues and had done committee work on the Windsor Report. He brought both his pastoral and theological concerns and his knowledge of the "state of affairs" in the Anglican Communion.

It was at this presentation that a member of the search committee, who had not attended either of the other presentations, interrupted the proceedings to voice an angry protest that none of this process should be taking place until after a new rector had been called. The interim rector reminded the group that interim times are ideal opportunities to address issues so that a new rector is not blindsided by them at the start of a new ministry. She reassured the gathering that it was not as important whether the decision to bless same-sex unions was "yes" or "no" as it was that *we talked about it together and together came to a clear decision.* It is worth noting that until this occasion all sharing of opposing views had been conducted with remarkable respect and mutual compassion by all parties.

Following the last of the three presentations, the chair of the Sub-Committee on the Process for Determining Policy suggested that the date for the vestry to vote on the matter be postponed in order to give the vestry and parish more time for reflection. However, it was concluded that the initial timeline still made sense.

The Decision

Beginning in mid-April the parish leadership invited parishioners to provide feedback to the vestry and/or clergy. A number of responses came by email and letter; vestry persons interviewed others.

On May 18, 2005, following a time of quiet prayer and the Eucharist, the vestry considered all they had heard from parishioners, from the parish "conversations," and from the presentations. After being led in prayer by the interim rector, a member of the vestry made the following motion:

> *"After study, discussion, and prayers for guidance from the Holy Spirit, I move that this vestry, as the elected leadership of the congregation, approve Services of Blessing for Same Gender Relationships to be performed at St. Peter's Church at the discretion of the Rector and in accordance with the Standards of the Episcopal Diocese of Delaware."*

In the discussion that followed, it was noted that the bishops of the Episcopal Church had pledged in March that they would not authorize public rites for the blessing of same-sex unions nor bless such unions themselves until at least the 2006 General Convention. The bishop of Delaware was asked if this overrode the published Standards and he indicated that they did not, since there was no official rite involved and the Standards concerned pastoral response on the part of local congregations.

The vote taken was twelve to zero in favor of the motion. When someone said it was unanimous, there was objection from two vestry members who stated that it really wasn't a unanimous decision. Although they were personally opposed to having blessings at St. Peter's, they had voted yes, because they believed that it was the clear wish of the majority of the parish to do these blessings. They said they'd voted yes, overriding their own personal feelings, in order to respect the overall feeling of the parish. The vestry then reported the vote as 12–0, but the word unanimous was not used.

Aftermath

Following the vestry decision, the parish was informed and attention turned to the search for a new rector. St. Peter's called the Reverend Jeffery A. Ross, who determined that standards applied to heterosexual marriage would also apply to same-sex unions, in particular the decision that at least one of the persons being blessed must be a member of the parish.

In 2011 Delaware became a state in which civil unions of same-sex couples were authorized, and parishes where preparation had taken place were permitted by the diocese to have services blessing such civil unions. The form for such blessings is suggested by the diocese but not authorized. The expectation is that such blessings rightfully belong in the context of the celebration of the Eucharist. St. Peter's has been a place of such blessings and those blessings have enriched our common life.

In the process of deciding to bless same-sex unions, the parish lost several families and gained many more. It has been essentially a non-issue within the parish. St. Peter's has not become "the Gay

Church in Lewes," although conservative members of other churches have described it as such. The process has taught us a lot about the need to practice inclusion on many levels. It has also forced us to look again at the sadness of our divisions from others in the community on the basis of race and status.

During this period—roughly from 2003 to the present—St. Peter's has also become a more mission-conscious parish, both on a local and a worldwide level. It has made remarkable strides in new engagements with the Jewish community and has begun wider spiritual friendships with Muslims, Hindus, and Buddhists. It has engaged anew the African American community in Lewes. The process we followed was a positive experience overall, becoming a model for the parish in that wider discussions of significant developments in the life of the parish are the norm. There are ongoing discussions of how St. Peter's will live out its growing sense that it is called to be a gathering place in the heart of Lewes for all the community. The process of education and conversation has also brought us new leadership in the parish, leadership that is renewed for the wider effort to make St. Peter's a focus for life in community in Lewes. We are now able to call ourselves "A Sanctuary in the Heart of Lewes."

✤ ✤ ✤

The Reverend Patricia Bird is a retired priest, volunteering with Meals on Wheels and Habitat for Humanity; she also serves on the Commission on Ministry in the Diocese of Delaware and is exploring mutual ministry for small churches. The Reverend Canon Mark Harris is an associate priest at St. Peter's, Lewes, writes on things Anglican and Episcopal, and offers practical support in Haiti and other venues.

CHAPTER 4

FredandBill

The Tale of a Couple and Their Parish

Martha Sterne

At St. Andrew's in Maryville, Tennessee, in 1998, Fred and Bill came to us as a package—FredandBill. The only gay couple in the parish—RonandJim—had invited FredandBill to church. They told me later that they were aware of the reputed tolerance of the congregation and they knew the beauty of the building and the gardens. They took a liking to me, but what sold them was the fellowship of the choir, which they joined immediately.

They made clear to me that they didn't want to make a fuss or have a political statement made out of their presence; they just wanted to be able to be part of the church in peace. By the time they got to us, they had been together forty-three or forty-four years.

Fred is huge, about 6'4", and bald with a deep, infectious laugh. His head moves in front of his body like the prow of a ship, and he has an inquiring half-smile on his face when he walks into the room. He was an internist who practiced medicine well into his eighties. He drove a big Cadillac well into his nineties; I hope he has quit by now, but I don't know.

Bill is short and quiet, a retired accountant, probably ten years younger than Fred. He became the church treasurer right after he was confirmed and stayed at his post until dementia came creeping in on cat's paws.

They met in New York when Bill was just finishing college and Fred was doing his residency, I think at St. Luke's Hospital. They decided to make their life together. It was totally beyond their imagination that their union could be blessed by a church, although early on they began a tradition of celebrating the day they met as their anniversary.

FredandBill began looking for a place to live in upper Manhattan. Their description of what happened surprised me. They were demoralized by several scalding rejections from potential landlords who took one look at them and said there was no room at the inn, so to speak. I thought New York City was way beyond this, certainly by the sixties. FredandBill were not partiers or swingers, so maybe the neighborhoods where they tried to rent were rigid. All these years later, I have wondered why Fred, who appears and actually is very dignified and macho, didn't just go by himself to look for their apartment, but that is not the way he rolls.

Two other truly disheartening things happened to them in New York. Fred landed in the hospital with a serious condition, and Bill had to pretend to be his brother or not get to see him. This humiliated them. Also, they started going to a mainline church—one of the big names—and somehow, in a very very early conversation with a pastor, they got the impression that the church only wanted their money. I don't believe that the pastor actually meant that. Do you? But time after time of experiencing being unwanted for their real selves, not to mention being uncelebrated—well, I imagine that being rejected becomes a way of hearing and seeing, no matter what people say.

FredandBill came south, of all places, and for the next forty years they lived their life and thanked God in their private ways for their union. Wherever they lived, their gardens were their pride and joy. They had friends and worked well and faithfully at their professions. But a community—of faith, of common prayer, of intentional, liturgical worship of God Almighty, of growing in Christ—that was missing.

Over the first few years of their entry into the church, not only did they join the choir and Bill become the treasurer, the two of them also took over the flower beds around the entrance to the church, which flourished under their care. Ivy grew up the walls of the church, beautiful old vines as thick as your ankle. I loved the way the ivy looked against the old bricks of the building, handmade on site by the original congregation of Quakers. FredandBill hated the ivy because it got in their flower beds, and, as they correctly pointed out, it was eating into the mortar between the bricks. One summer the ivy even climbed through a window and came to church.

Our running joke was that they would get the ivy down over my dead body. Actually, they got it stripped off about ten minutes after my car was outside the Maryville city limits on my way to a new job in Atlanta. They sent me a photo of the new ivy-less church and signed it on the back, "Love, FredandBill," with a big smiley face.

Over the years, a small, steady stream of young gay men, usually not long out of the Appalachian hills and hollers, would get introduced into their circle of friends, and sometimes come to church. Actually, FredandBill were some of our best evangelists to all sorts and conditions of people because they knew what it felt like to be on the outside looking in, and even harder, to feel this emptiness in your life and not know at all how to fill the God-shaped void.

Fred would say to me that he never thought that he would be able to be part of a Christian community, and he was so grateful, so grateful, he would say with tears in his eyes, for Fred and Bill truly found meaning and belonging in that place and with that community. Notice I did not write their names squished together in this last sentence because once we got to know them, we really loved Fred. We really loved Bill. And we really knew FredandBill just like we knew AnneandDick and TomandBeth.

The summer of 2003, we had a Bible study about human sexuality since the Episcopal Church was discussing Bishop Robinson's consecration. Fred came. Not Bill. It was a mixed group and we just went through different Bible stories about the human condition, really, and we looked in context at the texts that are cited by those who are disturbed by homosexuality. There was low-grade tension in the room. After all, when you are talking about a theology of human sexuality and you are reading scripture and you have a real live gay person in the room, can you continue just to tolerate homosexuals in a don't ask/don't tell kind of way or do you have to go deeper?

Jim, a conservative older man, took the risk and went deeper. He said he didn't believe in homosexuality and he thought it was a sin and that the Bible said it was, right there in black and white.

Fred made a noise way back in his nose and throat, "uuhmm-mmmhhhh." Not in a hostile kind of way, just in a taking-in-what-you-just-said-and-not-liking-it-much kind of way. He stood up. I'll never forget it. He stood up from the table and, stepping behind his chair, put his hands on the back of the chair. Remember he is 6'4". And then he said,

I am a homosexual.

I am not a mistake.

God made me and loves me.

And then he sat down. Long silence. I thought to myself, Fred just did Paul Tillich's "I am accepted" sermon in sixteen words. The class went on, but transfigured. We did go deeper, for we had been touched by an incarnation of the One in whom there is no east or west, no slave or free, no male or female, no gay or straight.

I wish I could say that the man who asked the question changed his mind, but I doubt it. What changed was the class, which is to say what changed was the church. Fred's words quietly reverberated through the men's group and the kitchen ladies and the Sunday school teachers and the vestry and the outreach folks. His words reverberated powerfully in the choir and out into the musically inclined community, even more of whom came to be with us. We became a church that didn't just tolerate gay folks. We became a church whose most powerful evangelist happened to be a gay eighty-plus-year-old, bald giant of a man named Fred, child of God and husband of Bill.

❖ ❖ ❖

Martha Sterne is writer-in-residence at Holy Innocents' Episcopal Church in Atlanta, Georgia. She is the author of Earthly Good *and* Alive and Loose in the Ordinary. *Her latest project is working with parishes and groups to co-create photo and video essays of holy moments and sacred stories.*

CHAPTER 5

What to Do[1]

Susan Russell

Grace to you and peace—and many thanks for the wonderful hospitality of this parish and pulpit! I am so very pleased to be with you this morning representing Claiming the Blessing: a national collaborative ministry committed to healing the rift between sexuality and spirituality in the church. Our focus right now is on the 2003 General Convention—the triennial gathering of the national Episcopal Church clan. It's an amazing thing, General Convention: kind of like that wonderful Broadway musical—*Brigadoon*—where every so many years the village emerges from the mists—only to fade away again until the next time.

This will be my fifth opportunity to participate in this uniquely Episcopal experience: what one colleague has called "part parliament, part bazaar, and part *My Big Fat Anglican Wedding*. My work for the last year has primarily focused on getting ready for the upcoming convention—traveling around the country sharing the hopes and dreams and goals the Claiming the Blessing collaborative has for

---

1. This sermon was preached by Susan Russell at Trinity Church, Santa Barbara, on July 13, 2003.

this church we love. I've been to Houston and Portland, San Diego and Boston, Nashville and Boulder, and lots of places in between. But now the orchestra is tuning up for the overture and the curtain is about to rise as our own Brigadoon—General Convention 2003—prepares to emerge from the mists in Minneapolis in just a little over two weeks. And so this morning is really the last stop on the road show.

It's a little like ending up back at home for me. I grew up in Santa Barbara—spent my high school and college years cruising State Street, hanging out at Ledbetter Beach—and avoiding attending church here at Trinity. It was nothing personal—I was avoiding attending church anywhere—part of what I now call my obligatory-young-adult-lapsed phase. My parents handled it just fine—they were more or less lapsed themselves—but my aunt Gretchen (who lived with us) found my heathen ways a source of great consternation—particularly, I think, because she'd tried too hard to be a "good influence" by taking me to Junior Altar Guild at the Cathedral.

Yes, our family was a great disappointment to Gretchen. So, in some ways, was this church family she loved. She died (and was buried from this church) a disgruntled Daughter of the King with a "Save the 1928 Prayer Book" bumper sticker on her car.

Years later, after I'd been ordained, I ran into one of her bridge buddies at a diocesan service. Giving me a big hug she said, "Oh, Gretchen would have been so proud!" Then she paused for a moment and said, "Well, at least I'd like to think she'd have come around by now!" And I think she would have come around, too, for she'd have certainly kept *coming* around; not even women priests and new prayer books would have driven her out of this church which was in many ways as much her family as we were.

So for me, *My Big Fat Anglican Wedding* is really the best General Convention descriptor after all. In the end I believe the Episcopal family of ours is as distinguished by its divergent opinions as it is by its common prayer: providing us with both our greatest strength and our greatest challenge. And as we prepare to gather in Minneapolis, of all the prayers ascending for the work we will do together over our ten days of legislative sessions, none has spoken to me so clearly of both those challenges and opportunities as the one we heard this morning:

> *O Lord, mercifully receive the prayers of your people who call upon you, and grant that they may know and understand what things they ought to do, and also may have grace and power faithfully to accomplish them; through Jesus Christ our Lord, who lives and reigns with you and the Holy Spirit, one God, now and for ever. Amen.*

Help us figure out what to *do*, then give us grace to *do* it. It brings to my mind the words of my favorite theologian, the African American Episcopalian and biblical scholar Verna Dozier. Verna said, "Don't tell me what you believe—tell me what difference it makes that you believe."

A prayer and a challenge we would be well served praying and hearing 365 days a year—not just this Fifth Sunday after Pentecost—"Proper 10" in the lectionary cycle—the day it's appointed to be read. But appointed it is—and so are the lessons for today. And it was in looking at those lessons for this morning through the lens of the Collect of the Day that I found both food for thought and strength for the journey—to General Convention and beyond.

Help us figure out what to *do*. That was Amos's challenge—the reluctant prophet called to speak truth to the political and religious institutions of his day.

> *This is what the Lord God showed me: the Lord was standing beside a wall built with a plumb line, with a plumb line in his hand. And the Lord said to me, "Amos, what do you see?" And I said, "A plumb line." Then the Lord said,*
>
> > *"See, I am setting a plumb line in the midst of my people*
> > > *Israel; I will never again pass them by;*
> > *the high places of Isaac shall be made desolate,*
> > *and the sanctuaries of Israel shall be laid waste,*
> > *and I will rise against the house of Jeroboam with the*
> > > *sword." (Amos 7:7-9)*

In seminary we were reminded that the prophet has two jobs: to comfort the afflicted—and to afflict the comfortable. Here Amos finds himself in the latter role—afflicting the comfortable leaders of Israel with the news that they were not measuring up to their high calling to be God's people in the world—and that all the sanctuaries and high places they could build were no substitute for aligning themselves with God's plumb line—with, in the words of the prophet Micah, God's "requirement": do justice, love mercy, and walk humbly with your God.

That his words were not received as good news by the recipients will not come as a surprise to anyone who has ever rattled the cages of power or challenged the status quo of the establishment. And I know this congregation well enough to know there are many here whose personal experience will bear that out. The powers that be were perfectly happy with the way it was, and the high priest invited

Amos to take his action elsewhere. Amos's reply? *"I am no prophet, nor a prophet's son; but I am a herdsman, and a dresser of sycamore trees, and the Lord took me from following the flock, and the Lord said to me, 'Go, prophesy to my people Israel'"* (Amos 7:14).

Amos knew what he was supposed to do: prophesy. And God gave him—a humble herdsman and dresser of sycamore trees—the grace and power to do it. His call was to speak the truth to power, and he did what he was sent to do. His words, which fell on deaf ears at the time, remain for us—centuries later—words of both encouragement and challenge: to speak the truth to power when we are called to—whether we feel qualified or not, whether it works or not.

The disciples in this morning's gospel were sent as well—sent by Jesus. He told them what to do: cast out unclean spirits. I love that he gave them an out—the "shake the dust off your feet" part as a last resort for anyone who refused to hear them—and that they didn't seem to need it: "They cast out many demons, and anointed with oil many who were sick and cured them" (Mark 6:13).

Like Amos before them, they were both told what to do and given grace and power to do it. And so have we.

I am heading to General Convention convinced that God has not only given us to understand what things we ought to do, but has also given us the grace and power to accomplish them. Claiming the Blessing is about so much more than the authorization of liturgies for the blessing of a tiny percentage of the Body of Christ already blessed by each other's love. It is about the Good News that the fuller inclusion of all the baptized into the Body of Christ is not an issue that will split the church but an opportunity that will move the church forward in mission and ministry, if we will claim it and proclaim it. It is about an opportunity for evangelism that will breathe new life into our work and our witness to those yearning to hear an alternative to the strident voices of the religious right who have for too long presumed to speak to the culture as representing Christian values. We have been given Good News to tell, and it's time to get on with the business of telling it.

Yes, there will be those who do not hear our news as good. Neither did the high priest in Israel, but that didn't stop Amos. Yes, there will be some who will refuse to hear what we have to say, but Jesus offers us the same option he offered the disciples when he sent them out in twos to heal in his name: shake the dust off your feet if you have to, but keep going. The journey is too important—the stakes are too high—the work you have been called to do is too important to be held hostage to those who will not hear the truth.

And the truth is there are some with power in this church determined to do nearly anything to keep it—including exploiting the fears of those who love this church by repeating over and over that rupture of the communion is inevitable.

Enough is enough. It's time for *us* to speak the truth as we know it. We are stronger than that. We have weathered greater than that. There is indeed room in this big fat Anglican faith of ours— this family of ours—for differing opinions and perspectives—even theologies and practices. Our primates—the heads of all the different national Anglican churches—have said so, declaring that they "respect the integrity of each other's provinces and dioceses, [and acknowledge] the responsibility of Christian leaders to attend to the pastoral needs of minorities in their care." Now that's a message of hope rather than fear—a blessing we claim far greater than any specific rites or any pending resolutions.

More words of wisdom from Verna Dozier: "Doubt is not the opposite of faith: fear is. Fear will not risk that even if I am wrong, I will trust that if I move today by the light that is given me, knowing it is only finite and partial, I will know more and different things tomorrow than I know today, and I can be open to the new possibility I cannot even imagine today."[2]

Jesus didn't call us to be "right"—he called us to be faithful. He called us to walk in love—with him and with each other. To believe in the power of love to cast out fear. To trust that the historic Anglican tradition we inherit can and will provide for us the "elbow room" we need to include all who seek to love and serve our Lord—all who desire to be fed by the holy food and drink of new and unending life we will soon share around this altar—all who seek to be vehicles of both God's blessing and abundant love.

We have been called to move forward in faith by the light we have in front of us—to claim the blessing of God's inclusive love and to offer the Good News of both the Gospel and the Episcopal Church to a world desperately in need it. We have work to do and the will to do it. And may the One who has given us the will to do these things give us as well the grace and power to accomplish them faithfully.

❖ ❖ ❖

The Reverend Canon Susan Russell, a life-long Episcopalian and native of Los Angeles, is a Senior Associate at All Saints Church in Pasadena, California, where she has been on staff since 2002. She has served on the National Board of Episcopal Church Women, is a past president of Integrity USA and a founding a member of the Human Rights Campaign Religion Council.

---

2. Verna J. Dozier, *The Dream of God: A Call to Return* (Cambridge, MA: Cowley Publications, 1991), 61.

CHAPTER 6

Making Room for Grace Dialogue

Eric H. F. Law

Some years ago, an Episcopal bishop asked me to create a dialogue curriculum to assist local church communities to discern their call to the ministry of hospitality. As I went about writing this curriculum, I realized that the first step of this process must deal with the fear of talking about this subject of sexuality. As denominational leaders across the church have been debating LGBT issues, including marriage and ordination for many years, local church communities have often had few opportunities to engage in constructive dialogue about sexuality in general and same-sex issues in particular. The curriculum that follows incorporates the technique I call Grace Margin, a conscious way of creating a gracious environment in which people's fear is lessened so that they may encounter the differing views of others. It is important to note that achieving mutual understanding is not about finding agreement. People in the Grace Margin can still disagree but with a deeper understanding of each other's experiences. Here are the techniques for creating a Grace Margin that I applied to the design for the dialogue curriculum:

1. *Negotiate for time:*[1] In the world in which we live, time is often perceived as a commodity. When there is a lack of time, most groups will instinctively move to function in legalistic and political ways. "Let's debate and vote on this and then go home because we do not have time to waste," they say. Grace begins with the commitment to offer our time to be with each other.

2. *Set parameters.*[2] State clearly what we will and will not do with the agreed-upon time. We need to state clearly that during the allotted time, we will not do that which is fearful to the people involved. We also need to say what we will do during this time that might be out of the ordinary, but important. This is an invitation to explore, to build new relationships and to consider different understandings and perspectives; it will not be business as usual.

3. *Introduce Dialogue Ground Rules:*[3] The Dialogue Ground Rules allow the Grace Margin to be upheld.

4. *Include diverse images of God:*[4] Any diverse community comes with diverse relationships with God. We need to enable people in the community to uphold and respect the different images of God that exist in the community. We are not talking about accepting all ideas of God indiscriminately. Within the Christian traditions and in the Bible alone, there are many diverse ideas of God. We simply need to know how to point to them

---

1. Eric H. F. Law, *Inclusion* (St. Louis: Chalice Press, 2000), 48–49.

2. Ibid., 59–66. For a full description of parameter setting in the context of a Process for Planned Change, see Eric H. F. Law, *Sacred Act, Holy Change* (St. Louis: Chalice Press, 2002), 104–110.

3. This version is modified from the first version of the Dialogue Ground Rules which were first published in Eric H. F. Law, *The Bush Was Blazing But Not Consumed* (St. Louis: Chalice Press, 1996), 85–98.

4. See Eric H. F. Law, *Inclusion* (St. Louis: Chalice Press, 2000), 67–82.

and invite people to explore together what this diversity means. We can raise up a diversity of God-images through prayers, songs, and Bible study for each gathering.

5. *Frame the gathering like a liturgy:* Finally, an effective way to create a Grace Margin is to design each gathering as if it were a liturgy. Using elements from a recognizable pattern of worship can remind participants that everything we do in this time and place is worship—our listening and receiving from God, and our grateful responding to God.[5]

The following are the Introduction and the outline of the first of five sessions of the *Making Room for Grace* dialogue program. (For the full dialogue curriculum, contact the Kaleidoscope Institute through our website: *www.kscopeinstitute.org*.)

Introduction: Concerning the Dialogue Process

The *Making Room for Grace* dialogue process seeks to enable individuals to listen openly and communicate honestly with each other knowing that there will be differences in perspectives, assumptions, and even theologies. The dialogue process itself does not take a side on any of the issues that may surface; it serves to provide a gracious and spirit-filled environment in which participants can feel safe and free to engage each other in honest dialogue. In dialogue, there is always a possibility of growth and change as a result of increased understanding amongst the participants, but changing of people's perspectives and values is not a presumed outcome. All we

---

5. For a description of the liturgically based approach called form-center leadership, see Eric H. F. Law, *The Bush Was Blazing But Not Consumed* (St. Louis: Chalice Press, 1996), 112–119.

ask is for participants to be open to where the Holy Spirit might be leading them.

In this spirit, the dialogue process is written in the form of the liturgy of Holy Eucharist. Each session begins with prayers. Then we study Holy Scriptures together as the liturgy of the Word. To minimize the use of Holy Scripture as a political tool, we do not choose particular scriptural passages to go with the themes of the sessions. Instead, we simply study the Gospel lesson of the upcoming Sunday according to the Revised Common Lectionary. In other words, this curriculum does not focus on the interpretation of various scriptural passages dealing specifically with "sexual minorities."

After the study of Holy Scripture, we move into a dialogue process. Then we pray together in the Prayers of the People, we offer each other the Peace of Christ and we share in the Eucharist before being dismissed.

Priest

A priest of the church community must be present for every session as the celebrant for the Eucharist. However, the priest must not be perceived by the rest of the participants as an expert, especially in the Bible study time. She or he must participate in the dialogue process as an equal to the rest.

Overview of the Dialogue Process

Session 1: Orientation and setting the parameters of the dialogue process

Session 2: Understanding the "majority myth" about sex, sexual orientation, identity, and relationship in our society

Session 3: What do we know about "sexual minorities" in our midst?

Session 4: Encountering people who consider themselves "sexual minorities" and Christians

Session 5: Having participated in this dialogue process, what do we do now as a church community?

Preparation

In order to facilitate this dialogue process, a team will need to first experience this full program themselves and then decide as a team where modification may be helpful to fit the specific personality, needs, and interests of the community.

For Session 4 to be most productive, the facilitators will need to invite individuals who consider themselves "sexual minorities" and are willing to share openly their life experiences and faith. If the local church community does not include such individuals, the diocese may have suggestions. Exposure to real people who identified themselves as "sexual minorities" is crucial in this dialogue process.

Setting

The sessions should ideally be held in a large, bright room with wall space for the display of flip-chart papers. There should be enough chairs for all participants.

Size of Group

This process is designed for a group of twenty-four to thirty-two adults.

Facilitators

Four facilitators are required for this program. If you have more or fewer participants than noted above, plan for one facilitator for every eight participants. Facilitators should have basic skills in leading small-group dialogue.

Session 1:
Orientation and Setting the Parameters of the Dialogue Process

Goals

To introduce the participants to the dialogue process

To explore the parameters within which the dialogue process will take place

To invite participants to commit themselves to participate in the full five-session dialogue program

Preparation

1. Read the Gospel lesson for the Sunday after this dialogue session. Determine a second reflection question relevant to the subject of this session.

2. Create wall charts for participants to respond to the following questions:

   If we are to discuss the topic of sex, what are your fears?

   What will help you participate more fully in this dialogue?

Process

    I. Opening Prayer

    II. Purpose of Gathering

    III. Dialogue Ground Rules (see handout)

    IV. Explanation of Mutual Invitation (see handout)

    V. Kaleidoscope Bible Study (see handout)

    VI. Break

    VII. Setting the Parameters for the Dialogue Process
Discussion Questions:

> If we are to discuss the topic of sex, what are your fears?
>
> What will help you participate more fully in this dialogue?
>
> Arrive at a set of mutually agreeable statements of what the group will and will not do during the dialogue process.

    VIII. Commitment for Future Participation

    IX. Reflection on the Experience (10 minutes)

    X. Prayer of the People

    XI. The Peace

    XII. Holy Eucharist

    XIII. Blessings and Dismissal

Session 1 Handouts

Dialogue Ground Rules

We are not here to debate who is right or who is wrong. We are here to experience true dialogue in which we strive to communicate honestly and listen actively and openly to each other. We invite you to open your hearts and minds to experience new ideas, feelings, situations, and people, even though at times the process may be uncomfortable.

Our facilitators are not experts. Their role is to provide a structure and process by which we can better communicate with each other.

We recognize that we might have preconceived assumptions and perceptions about others—some are conscious; some are unconscious. We invite you to be aware of how they influence the way you listen and interpret others' words and actions. We also invite you to be aware of how these assumptions affect the way you speak and act in the group. In doing so, we can better maintain our respect for and acceptance of ourselves and others as valuable human beings.

We invite you to take responsibility for what you say and what you say on behalf of a group. We also invite you to speak with words that others can hear and understand and whenever possible, use specific personal examples that relate to the topic being discussed.

We invite you to expand your listening sense to include not just words, but also feelings being expressed, non-verbal communication such as body language, and different ways of using silence.

We invite you to take responsibility for your own feelings as they surface. Feelings may be triggered by particular words or actions, but they may or may not be directly related to the particular interaction. When this happens, simply communicate that feeling without blaming others.

In doing so, members of the group can hear and learn constructively the consequences of their words and actions.

We invite you to hold the personal information shared here in confidence because only in this way can we feel free to say what is in our minds and hearts.

Mutual Invitation

In order to ensure that everyone who wants to share has the opportunity to speak, we will proceed in the following way:

> *The leader or a designated person will share first. After that person has spoken, he or she then invites another to share. Who you invite does not need to be the person next to you. After the next person has spoken, that person is given the privilege to invite another to share. If you are not ready to share yet, say "I pass for now" and we will invite you to share later on. If you don't want to say anything at all, simply say "pass" and proceed to invite another to share. We will do this until everyone has been invited.*

❖ ❖ ❖

Eric F. Law is founder and Executive Director of the Kaleidoscope Institute, the mission of which is to create inclusive and sustainable churches and communities. For more than 20 years, he has provided transformative and comprehensive training and resources for churches and ministries in all the major church denominations in the United States and Canada. He is the author of seven books including The Wolf Shall Dwell with the Lamb *and his latest,* Holy Currencies: Six Blessings for Sustainable Missional Ministries.

Kaleidoscope Bible Study Process

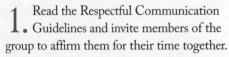

1. Read the Respectful Communication Guidelines and invite members of the group to affirm them for their time together.

2. Inform participants that the Bible passage will be read three times. After each reading, participants will be invited to share their reflections.

✤ FIRST READING

3. Invite participants to capture a word, a phrase or image when listening to the passage the first time.

4. Invite someone to read the passage.

5. Take a moment of silence to capture a word, a phrase or image that stood out from the passage for them.

6. Using Mutual Invitation, invite each person to share his or her word, phrase or image briefly. (*This should take no more than five minutes.*)

✤ SECOND READING

7. Invite participants to consider the second question appointed for this passage. (*Facilitator should prepare ahead of time a question that is relevant to participants' context.*)

8. Invite someone to read the passage a second time.

9. Take a moment of silence to reflect on the question.

10. Using Mutual Invitation, invite each person to share his or her reflection.

✤ THIRD READING

11. Invite participants to consider the following question while listening to the passage again.

"What does God invite you to do, be, or change through this passage?"

12. Invite someone to read the passage a third time.

13. Take a moment of silence to reflect on the question.

14. Using Mutual Invitation, invite each person to share his or her reflection.

✤ CIRCLE PRAYER

15. End the session with a prayer circle:

Invite participants to join hands in a circle. Invite each person to mentally complete the sentences:

I thank God today . . .

I ask God today . . .

The leader will begin by sharing his or her prayers. After he or she has shared, the leader then squeezes the hand of the person to the right. That will be the signal for the next person to share his or her prayers. If the person does not want to share, he or she can simply pass the pulse to the next person. When the pulse comes back to the leader, he or she can begin the Lord's Prayer and invite everyone to join in.

CHAPTER 7

A Guide for Dialogue[1]

Episcopal Diocese of San Diego

The task force members gave each other the gifts of time and personal commitment as we approached the task before us. We began discussion gently, with guidelines and ground rules, taking care to balance the initial small groups in terms of general point of view, clergy, and laity. Step by step, we grew into a community of mutual respect and support that faced difficult and controversial subjects directly. With great intention, we came to recognize the presence of the Holy Spirit.

Our willingness to address the difficult, controversial subjects candidly, without blame or defense, became the blessing of our work. We became better informed and more sensitive and respectful to each other as persons of common faith.

---

1. This guide appeared as an appendix to the Report of the Task Force on Holiness in Relationships and the Blessing of Same-Sex Relationships issued by the Episcopal Diocese of San Diego in June 2009, pp. 72–74. The theologically diverse task force was authorized by a 2008–09 Resolution of the Diocesan Convention. It was appointed by the bishop and included clergy and lay people reflective of the diocese. The goal of the task force was to study holiness in relationships and blessings in churches of this diocese from the perspectives of holy scripture, church history, and tradition; practical, pastoral, and sacramental theology; and the movement of the Holy Spirit; and then to prepare a written report to the 2009 Diocesan Convention. The editor wishes to extend thanks to the Right Reverend James R. Mathes for permission to include this appendix with its excellent questions.

It is our recommendation and hope that you will invest in a similar process: address the difficult subjects, seek understanding (not necessarily agreement) of other points of view, and nurture your community. We pray that you will do this in love for the Episcopal Church and your call to live out the Gospel of Jesus Christ.

Guidelines for Discussion

- Be as committed to listening to others as to speaking for yourself.
- There are not "right" answers or "wrong" answers, no winners, no losers.
- Share your ideas and feelings—do not debate or insist on proving your point.
- The most important part of the discussion is your respect for each other.

Study Questions

Scripture

1. How do we determine which translation of scripture to use to support our study and interpretation?
2. Is it appropriate to interpret scripture on the basis of what was "not said"?
3. After learning the different ways of interpreting scripture, which way do you find to be most helpful for yourself?
4. After reading the different views about scriptural texts, which of these particularly resonate with you?

5. What does scripture say about homosexual or same-sex relations?

6. What does scripture say about heterosexual or opposite-sex relations?

Holy Relationships

7. What kind of relationships can be holy—only opposite-sex relationships, or would you include same-sex relationships?

8. If a same-sex relationship does not include sexual intercourse, can it be holy?

9. If an opposite-sex relationship includes premarital or extra-marital sexual intercourse, can it be holy?

10. How would the blessing of a couple in a committed relationship differ from the marriage of a couple in a committed relationship?

The Church

11. What does "blessing" mean to you?

12. How has the Church's teaching about marriage changed over the centuries? What has stayed the same? What has prompted change?

13. Should the clergy of our diocese dispense with being the agents of civil marriage and focus only on blessing holy relationships, regardless of whether civil marriage has occurred?

14. If "local option" to conduct same-sex blessings were allowed by General Convention and the Diocese of San Diego, what should the discernment process be *in each congregation* to determine the appropriateness of conducting these blessings?

15. Should the decision to bless a relationship require the same standards and pastoral oversight as a request to conduct a marriage ceremony?

Personal Reflection

16. The Episcopal Church bases its faith on the "three-legged stool" of scripture, tradition, and reason. What is the importance of each? Is any one more important than any other?

17. What experiences have you had that influenced you to look again at the relationships of gay couples within the church?

18. What have you learned from your study? What have you learned from your discussion? Into which topics would you like to delve more deeply?

19. Has this study helped you to understand different perspectives on these issues?

20. How can we live in community with each other when we disagree about these important matters?

CHAPTER 8

Who Are Our Sisters and Brothers?

Discussing Same-Sex Blessings in the Anglican Communion

Ruth Meyers

As a deputy to General Convention in 2009 and 2012, I was delighted to vote in 2009 to direct the Standing Commission on Liturgy and Music to collect and develop theological and liturgical resources for blessing same-sex relationships and then in 2012 to authorize those newly developed resources for use in the Episcopal Church. These votes were complex. Many in the Episcopal Church have expressed concern that fuller welcome and inclusion of lesbian, gay, bisexual, and transgender (LGBT) people would harm relationships in the Anglican Communion. Yet I believe that *both* the rich diversity of the Anglican Communion *and* the Episcopal Church's growing acknowledgment and embrace of its LGBT members are evidence of the work of the Holy Spirit.

My perspective on the Anglican Communion has been shaped by my experience of the International Anglican Liturgical Consultation. I still remember the first meeting I attended. In August 1991, sixty-four Anglican liturgists from twenty-two provinces of the Anglican Communion gathered in Toronto, Canada, to discuss Christian initiation. I had never heard my native language spoken with so many accents!

Some of the participants were bishops, some were members of their province's liturgical commission, still others were liturgical scholars. As a young scholar still finishing her doctoral study of the Episcopal Church's development of baptism and confirmation in the 1979 Book of Common Prayer, it was eye-opening to hear so many different perspectives on this central aspect of Christian life. In the 1979 book the Episcopal Church had agreed that baptism is full initiation by water and the Holy Spirit into Christ's Body the Church (p. 298) and thus is the basis for admission to communion. But many churches in the Anglican Communion continued the inherited pattern that required confirmation before communion.

In our discussions in Toronto in 1991, we listened carefully to one another, seeking to understand not only the wisdom of our heritage but also the insights of contemporary liturgical scholarship. By the end of the week we agreed to recommend to provinces of the Anglican Communion that baptism is complete sacramental initiation and leads to participation in the Eucharist. As we talked about the practice of confirmation, a bishop from Africa reported that there were so many confirmands at some services in his diocese that at times he needed priests to assist him in administering the rite. So in Toronto we also agreed to recommend that a bishop may delegate the pastoral rite of confirmation to a priest.

Since that 1991 meeting, I've participated in most of the biennial meetings of the International Anglican Liturgical Consultation. I have broken bread with colleagues from around the world at elegant banquet tables and in spartan dining halls. We have celebrated Eucharist together under a tree on a hillside in England, in conference rooms from Prague to India, and in the crypt at Canterbury Cathedral. My conversations over the years have broadened my understanding not only of Anglican liturgy but also of the daily lived experience of Anglican communities in vastly different contexts. Over the years, as I've prayed for dioceses and bishops in the Anglican Cycle of Prayer, I am vividly aware of particular individuals and their needs and concerns.

Thus, when the 2009 General Convention directed the Standing Commission on Liturgy and Music to invite theological reflection from throughout the Anglican Communion as it collected and developed theological and liturgical resources for blessing same-sex relationships, I knew that the International Anglican Liturgical Consultation (IALC) was an appropriate place for such reflection. The IALC was scheduled to meet in Canterbury in August 2011, and its steering committee gave the Episcopal Church a half-day on the agenda to present the work in progress.

Over my years of participation in the IALC, I had come to appreciate the importance of careful preparation for conversation across difference. Diversities of cultures and theological perspectives sometimes led to heated clashes. The place of same-sex couples in the life and ministry of the church has been an especially divisive matter in the Anglican Communion. I expected that it could be so at an IALC meeting as well.

Several months before the Canterbury meeting, the steering committee met with me and Tom Ely, bishop of Vermont and a member of the Standing Commission on Liturgy and Music, to prepare for our presentation to the IALC meeting. We spent much of our conversation that day not in planning but in talking about the work of the commission, the process that we were following, and the theological and liturgical principles guiding our work. The Steering Committee agreed to assist us by sending out materials in advance and assigning participants to small groups that would each include a cross-section of different provinces.

A few weeks before the IALC meeting in August 2011, Bishop Ely and I sent a letter and material for registrants to read. Our letter began, "For more than thirty years the Episcopal Church has been in a church-wide discernment process about how we welcome and provide pastoral care for our gay and lesbian members." We cited the 1976 General Convention resolution that declares that homosexual persons are children of God and the 2009 resolution that prompted our work. We included several attachments, which we asked people to read in advance of the meeting:

1. The 1976 and 2009 General Convention resolutions

2. General Convention Resolution 2000-D039, which acknowledges "couples in the Body of Christ and in this Church who are living in other life-long committed relationships" (i.e., other than marriage) and sets forth the expectation that "such relationships will be characterized by fidelity, monogamy, mutual affection and respect, careful, honest communication, and the holy love which enables those in such relationships to see in each other the image of God"

3. General Convention Resolution 2003-C051, which recognizes "that local faith communities are operating within the bounds of our common life as they explore and experience liturgies celebrating and blessing same-sex unions"

4. A one-page statement of theological principles, which the Commission had developed early in the triennium and continued to revise as its work proceeded

5. A one-page statement of principles for evaluating liturgical materials, which the Commission developed to facilitate its work of assessing the resources it collected as well as the material it developed.

After we arrived in Canterbury, we had a few days before our appointed time on the agenda. This allowed us an opportunity to identify facilitators and scribes for each small group and meet with these leaders to clarify their roles and responsibilities.

Our design blended small-group process and plenary sessions. Tom Ely began with a presentation on his context as bishop of Vermont, a state that has had civil unions for same-sex couples since 2000, and civil marriages since 2009. He continued by talking about the context of the Episcopal Church and the conversations we've been having about the place of same-sex individuals and couples in the life and ministry of the church for several decades now. He reflected on our understanding of this work as part of engaging mission. I picked up the story, talking about the legislative history and the work then underway in the Standing Commission on Liturgy and Music. I reported that the one-page theological principles they had received were a summary of a fifty-page document still being developed. We distributed the one-page principles that had been sent in advance, along with some discussion questions for small groups. We asked the groups to consider whether the theological principles were rooted in scripture and historical Christian traditions, including Anglican tradition. We also asked how well the

principles addressed questions people in their provinces were asking, and we invited their questions and recommendations for the
Standing Commission on Liturgy and Music.

When we returned to the plenary after these small-group conversations, we did a role-play of a draft of the liturgy for blessing
same-sex couples. The commission had done similar role-plays in
its work. By engaging the proposed texts as prayer, even though we
were not actually blessing a couple in a covenantal relationship, we
were able to imagine how an assembly might experience the liturgy.
In the international meeting, we hoped that actually experiencing
the liturgy would invite participants to respond to a concrete experience. After enacting the liturgy, we once again sent participants into
small groups with discussion questions, this time accompanied by
the principles for evaluating liturgical materials. We invited them
to reflect on their experience of the liturgy as corporate prayer. We
asked whether the liturgy and the liturgical principles reflected
Anglican liturgical sensibilities and whether the liturgy appeared
consistent with the theological principles they had discussed earlier.
We invited their questions and recommendations for the Standing
Commission on Liturgy and Music.

During each small-group session, the scribes took careful notes,
which were later conveyed to the Standing Commission on Liturgy
and Music as it completed its work on the resources. Our goal was
not primarily to convey information that could be reported to other
provinces in the Communion but rather to learn how leaders from
other parts of the Communion perceived our work. What insights
could they offer that would improve our work? Did they have questions or concerns that we could address as we completed work on
the material? For example, we learned that the term "household"

was not sufficiently specific about the nature of the relationship to be blessed; explaining that the Episcopal Church is blessing monogamous, lifelong, committed relationships helped allay fears and correct misconceptions.

During that structured time of reflection as well as informal conversations throughout that IALC meeting, I heard many stories from different parts of the Communion. Some provinces are actively engaging the question of blessing same-sex couples and related matters of the place of LGBT people in the life and ministry of the church. While many are not, even in some of these provinces there is quiet acceptance of LGBT people in their midst. Some provinces look to the Episcopal Church to help address some of the issues; others think we have moved way too fast. All of those views, and more, were represented in that IALC meeting in August 2011.

No one was absent when the Episcopal Church was given time on the agenda, though it was an optional session. People listened respectfully. They asked questions, some hard questions, especially in small groups. In so doing, they engaged the process, and so showed great respect for the Episcopal Church.

Our conversations that day were one small but significant opportunity to build relationships in the Anglican Communion. Participants from the Episcopal Church offered stories of our church's growing acceptance of the blessing of same-sex relationships as part of our common life. With our sisters and brothers from throughout the Anglican Communion, we explored the theological principles that the Standing Commission on Liturgy and Music was developing and examined a draft of a new liturgy. Occasions like the International Anglican Liturgical Consultation thus enable us to address difficult questions from our various perspectives and so strengthen our ties as brothers and sisters in Christ, knit together by the Holy Spirit.

❖ ❖ ❖

Ruth Meyers is Hodges-Haynes Professor of Liturgics and Dean of Academic Affairs at Church Divinity School of the Pacific, and is Chair of the Episcopal Church Standing Commission on Liturgy and Music. She is currently working on a book about liturgy and mission.

CHAPTER 9

Bent Toward Justice

Emerging Generations
and the Inevitability of Inclusion

Stephanie Spellers

In a recent gathering of mission- and evangelism-minded Episcopalians, I ran a highly unscientific study. "How many of you were born after 1976?" Nearly all of the sixty-five people present raised their hands. "That was the year the General Convention of The Episcopal Church first declared its full pastoral support for lesbian and gay people," I told them. "In your lifetime, this church has been on record supporting the lives, ministries, and loves of lesbian, gay, bisexual, and transgendered people."

No one seemed surprised. Instead, most shrugged as if to say, "Well, how else would a church be?"

Or take my dear friend Glen, who is single, white, straight, and age thirty-three. He volunteers faithfully for a variety of organizations and serves as an assistant district attorney in one of Boston's toughest neighborhoods. He is easily one of the most generous and compassionate people I know. He is also an atheist who incongruously likes hanging out at church.

He told me about a recent visit to a church where a work friend was singing. After he had raved about the music and preaching, I said—almost in passing—"It's too bad many of the people we both love couldn't make a home there."

"Why?" he asked.

"Because they're gay," I reminded him.

His eyes got bigger and he shook his head. "Do churches still do that? Is that possible? What are they thinking?" he asked with no judgment, just sheer wonder. "I mean, I guess I've heard of it, but I just can't imagine, in our society, in this day, saying people couldn't get married or be part of a group because they're gay."

These are only anecdotes, but the hard numbers in study after study support the same conclusion:[1] people born after 1965 are unequivocal regarding the full embrace of lesbian, gay, bisexual, and transgender people. And they reject churches, at least in part, if they think we are anti-female, anti-reason, or anti-homosexual.

The research proves it. The daily lives of people under forty illustrate it. The present may be a time for struggle, dialogue, and reconciliation around human sexuality, but the long arc of the universe is bending toward justice. No church that hopes to share the good news of God in Christ among emerging generations will be able to do so while denying full embrace based on sexual orientation.

---

1. See David Kinnaman, *You Lost Me: Why Young Christians Are Leaving Church . . . and Rethinking Faith* (Grand Rapids, MI: Baker Books, 2011); David Kinnaman and Gabe Lyons, *unChristian: What a New Generation Really Thinks About Christianity . . . and Why it Matters* (Grand Rapids, MI: Baker Books, 2007); and "Generations at Odds: The Millennial Generation and the Future of Gay and Lesbian Rights," Public Religion Research Institute (October 2011, *http://publicreligion.org/research/2011/08/generations-at-odds*).

What Is at Stake?

If this is true, there is a lot more at stake as the Episcopal Church turns increasingly more inclusive.

Yes, as many have claimed, these moves are part and parcel of living into our baptismal promise to "seek and serve Christ in all persons" and to "strive for justice and peace among all people, and respect the dignity of every human being."

But we live that covenant in a mission context. In this American context, gay marriage statutes are hitting the books in state after state. Nearly two-thirds of people born after 1981 say they support same-sex marriage, double the percentage of their elders in the Silent Generation, born between 1928 and 1945.[2] Meanwhile, about one-third of Millennials say they have no religious affiliation at all (call them the "Nones"), compared to not quite 10 percent of their Silent elders and only 21 percent of Generation Xers born between 1965 and 1980.[3]

In this context, church is no longer the no-brainer it was even two or three generations ago. Now, equal rights and full inclusion is the no-brainer, and church is the anomaly. What is at stake in *this* context? The very proclamation of the good news of Jesus Christ.

We live among entire generations who simply cannot hear any church that does not affirm the only religious tenet many know: that God is love and God loves everyone. Some faith community rooted in that essential truth must step out to grow relationship with these emerging generations.

---

2. "Ten Years of Changing Attitudes on Gay Marriage," Pew Forum on Religion and Public Life (November 2012, *http://features.pewforum.org/gay-marriage-attitudes*).

3. "'Nones' on the Rise," Pew Forum on Religion and Public Life (October 2012, *http://www.pewforum.org/unaffiliated/nones-on-the-rise.aspx*).

The ground is fertile. If we are worried that young people simply do not want to hear news from us, good or otherwise, that is simply not true. They might not like church much, but they are rather fond of Jesus. Granted, many imagine him to be a nice, Santa Claus-like guy who bears little resemblance to the incarnate God. But there is also a purity and clarity to the expectations these onlookers place on us.

They know Jesus stood for love: of self and neighbor (and God, first of all). They want to see us loving in action. They have heard that Jesus stood with outcasts. They wonder why we seem so anxious to get away from anyone who might qualify as one. Some even guess that Jesus died while turning certain systems upside down. So why do Christians get so nervous about change in our own systems?

Emerging generations are watching and listening. They are waiting for good news that connects and speaks faithfully into their own lives and calls them to greater life. We have the opportunity to proclaim and embody it.

Tell Me More About This Jesus

Jesus knew how to preach that kind of good news. It sounded good to his contemporaries, and it would sound just as good today:

> He stood up to read, and the scroll of the prophet Isaiah was given to him. He unrolled the scroll and found the place where it was written:
>
> "The Spirit of the Lord is upon me,
> because he has anointed me
> to bring good news to the poor.

He has sent me to proclaim release to the captives
and recovery of sight to the blind,
to let the oppressed go free,
to proclaim the year of the Lord's favor."

And he rolled up the scroll, gave it back to the attendant, and sat
down. . . . Then he began to say to them, "Today this scripture
has been fulfilled in your hearing." (Luke 4:16b–21)

Jesus knew the pain of the people around him, and he knew the systems—including religious ones—that had for generations added burdens to the backs of already bent people. He consistently declared freedom for the ones who were held captive, sight for those who had been blind, favor for those who were poor and forgotten. Where he saw people with privilege, like the rich young man, he loved them enough to invite them to release their attachments, share with the poor and follow him.

I have to believe that, as he gazes on the worldwide community called Christians, Jesus sees the oppressed underclass of lesbian, gay, bisexual, and transgender people and wants freedom and favor for them. This freedom is not mere affirmation so that people can "feel good" about themselves. It is freedom to enter into the heart of God, giving our lives away for love of the world, just as he did. Jesus wants all of us to be forgiven and free so that we can all be servants, lovers, healers, and prophets for the kingdom of God.

Jesus turned no one away from that movement. And while he invited people to drop their old lives and follow him, he was more concerned with change and self-emptying that resulted in generosity, forgiveness, hospitality, reconciliation, and humility. Nothing of the gospel record advocates for lying to yourself and the world in a way that makes you less able to serve him.

That isn't just good news. It's the best news imaginable.

More Than a Trend

Clearly, there is far more at stake here than being hip, trendy, or—God forbid—more "relevant." Those of us born after 1965 were raised on television, social media, sophisticated marketing, and targeted messaging. We pride ourselves on being able to read a fake from miles away. If you are just following a trend, trying to be "cool," supporting gay marriage, or blessing unions because it is the thing to do, we are not impressed. Make the case with your whole heart, and then live it out.

This takes us well beyond the proof-texting and Bible gymnastics that mark too many discussions between right and left. It forces Episcopalians to make our practice and proclamation around LGBT inclusion part of our practice and proclamation of the good news of God in Jesus Christ. If it is not, then it will always ring hollow or faint . . . to young adults who are suspicious of the church *and* to faithful brothers and sisters who are on the fence about human sexuality.

But every time we go public and proclaim the good news with our hearts, souls, and voices, God is glorified. Every time one of our churches hosts a blessing of a same-sex union or marriage, some young person who thought God had nothing to do with her life might just give God another chance. Every time a General Convention affirms the full humanity, giftedness, and Christian witness of another outcast, some young onlooker may do a double-take. "That's the kind of church I want to know about." And we will be ready to share the full story of good news in Christ as we have received it.

This is the arc of the universe, the arc of God's activity throughout human history and beyond. Emerging generations are already aligned with it. We are simply moving our churches and communities to join them and join God.

✣ ✣ ✣

Stephanie Spellers is the Canon for Missional Vitality in the Diocese of Long Island, where she works to stir mission with emerging cultures across Brooklyn, Queens, and Long Island. She was the founding priest for The Crossing community at St. Paul's Cathedral in Boston and is the author of Radical Welcome: Embracing God, The Other, and the Spirit of Transformation.

CHAPTER 10

The Amazing Grace
of Same-Sex Blessings

Patrick S. Cheng

What is the strongest theological argument in favor of same-sex blessings? The answer, I contend, is that such relationships are *visible signs of God's grace*—an amazing kind of one-way love that is a pure gift and cannot be earned. I've come to this realization based upon over twenty years of being together with my husband, Michael, through our ups and downs, and for better or for worse.

Same-sex blessings are sacramental because they are a reflection of the larger grace-filled relationship between God and humanity. The classical theological definition of a sacrament—including baptism, Eucharist, and marriage—is that it is a visible and external sign of God's invisible grace. Same-sex blessings are holy because they are vehicles in which we can experience and gain a deeper understanding of God's unconditional love for us—a love that is, in the end, unmerited and unearned.

Michael and I have experienced a healthy dose of grace in our relationship over the last two decades. First of all, falling in love itself is an act of grace. As most of us have discovered, one simply cannot force another person to fall in love with her or him (that is, outside of the world of Shakespearean comedies and magic love potions). Love—whether same-sex or opposite-sex—is a manifestation of God's amazing grace precisely because it cannot be planned or earned. Love is not just a matter of works, but rather of grace.

I still marvel at the fact that Michael and I met through a personals ad in *Bay Windows*, the Boston-area lesbian, gay, bisexual, and transgender (LGBT) newspaper. What are the odds that this California-raised Chinese American man would find his Massachusetts-raised Irish American life partner in this way? Michael and I often say that we met, sight unseen, for a first date in Harvard Square over twenty years ago and never stopped talking. How could our relationship not be a matter of God's grace?

When Michael and I celebrated our Holy Union in the summer of 2000 at the Church of Saint Luke in the Fields in Greenwich Village, New York City, it was a profound moment that bore witness to God's amazing grace in our lives. Walking down the aisle with Michael in procession with the thurifer, crucifer, choir, and other ministers, I wasn't sure what to expect. Looking back on that day, however, I now realize that Michael and I were irrevocably changed—some might say ontologically changed—by the act of giving thanks to God in the presence of our family members, friends, co-workers, and parishioners.

Second, and more importantly, my relationship with Michael has survived (and grown!) because of the grace, or unmerited gift, of forgiveness. Over the last two decades, we have both forgiven each other for transgressions big and small, despite the fact that the other might actually be at fault and not "deserve" to be forgiven. I believe these graced moments of forgiveness are a reflection of the larger grace that marks the fundamental relationship between God and humanity.

Indeed, as Augustine of Hippo and Martin Luther have reminded us, grace is the central theme of the Bible, and, for that matter, of Christian theology. The parable of the prodigal child—who is accepted unconditionally by his father with open arms, despite leaving home, squandering his inheritance, and living with pigs—is all about grace. Similarly, God's gift to us of making human flesh divine in the incarnation—despite our propensity to turn our backs on God, from the Garden of Eden to the present—is also about grace.

As a queer theologian, seminary professor, and ordained minister, I have witnessed the gift of God's amazing grace reflected in countless same-sex relationships over the years. These relationships—some of which have lasted decades longer than mine—are nothing short of miraculous in light of the hatred and rejection that many same-sex couples have experienced from their families, churches, work colleagues, and local communities.

I have also witnessed how God's amazing grace has changed many people—particularly from communities of color—who were at one time afraid of LGBT people and have since become our strong allies. When I first came out to my mother in the late 1980s, she was horrified. "What will our family and friends think?," she asked me. She begged me not to tell my father and grandmother out of a concern that they would suffer greatly from the news. For many years, my mom lived in a place of fear, isolation, and shame.

Over time, however, God's amazing grace has worked wonders in my mom's life. Not only did she proudly attend our Holy Union (as did my father, who has since passed away), but she has embraced

Michael as her son-in-law. Around fifteen years ago, my mom marched in her first LGBT Pride parade. Three years ago, she spoke at a press conference in New York City about the need for Chinese American communities to love and accept their LGBT members. And just last summer, my mom filmed a public-service announcement for Chinese American parents who are struggling to accept their LGBT children.

It's surprising to me that the leaders of the religious right—including Protestant fundamentalists, Roman Catholic bishops, and Mormon leaders—have overlooked (or ignored) the centrality of grace in their reflections upon same-sex relationships. Their view that such relationships are inherently sinful, based upon notions of procreation and the complementarity of sexual organs, is an insult to the larger Christian message about God's extravagant grace-filled relationship with humanity. By focusing so closely upon the trees, they lose sight of the larger forest that is God's amazing grace.

Ironically, by restricting blessings to opposite-sex couples, the religious right is acting just like the narrow-minded zealots who were condemned by St. Paul in his New Testament letters. (Such zealots insisted that Christians had to follow specific religious rules like circumcision in order to attain salvation.) The religious right is proclaiming a gospel of works and not of grace. Its myopic view of same-sex relationships is a failure of not only the theological imagination, but also the theological virtues of faith, hope, and love.

It is time that we challenge the false dichotomy that same-sex relationships can only be supported on the basis of secular rights-based arguments, and that they must be opposed on the basis of the Christian faith. In my view, the strongest argument in support of same-sex blessings is that it is a visible and external sign of God's amazing grace—that is, a one-way love that is pure gift and cannot be earned—that flows extravagantly from God to humanity.

✛ ✛ ✛

Patrick S. Cheng is the Associate Professor of Historical and Systematic Theology at the Episcopal Divinity School in Cambridge, Massachusetts. He is the author of forthcoming Rainbow Theology: Bridging Race, Sexuality, and Spirituality *(Seabury, 2013). For more information about Patrick, see* http://www.patrickcheng.net.

CHAPTER 11

Variations on a Theological Theme

The Episcopal Church's Rite for Blessing a (Same-Sex) Covenant

Charles Hefling

A liturgical text is never just the script for a certain sort of theatrical performance. It is always also an expression of religious belief; arguably, for Episcopalians, the prime expression. The Anglican tradition to which we belong has typically found its theological identity in appointed forms of common prayer as much as in confessional formulas. To ask, then, what beliefs are being enacted, now that General Convention has authorized "provisional" use of a liturgy prescribing what is to be done and said at a service of blessing a same-sex union, is to ask no trifling question. It is to ask about the convictions, the character, the aims and aspirations of the community that has produced and endorsed this rite. What has the Episcopal Church said about itself by giving its blessing to such blessings?

It would be a mistake to suppose that what is most obvious about the new rite is what the rite obviously is. What is obvious is how closely the "shape of the liturgy" conforms to what used to be called "The Form of Solemnization of Matrimony" and is now, in the current Book of Common Prayer, "The Celebration and Blessing of a Marriage." A congregation gathers; a couple joins them; the presiding cleric explains why they are all there. After readings from scripture and a sermon, the couple is presented and the presider asks them each whether they truly mean to do what they have come for. Stated prayers are recited. Then each member of the couple takes the other's hand, repeats a solemn promise, gives a ring. Finally, on these promises and the couple who have made them, the presider pronounces a formal blessing. Nobody would say, as one of Shakespeare's characters does, "This looks not like a nuptial." That is just what it does look like.

Yet a nuptial it is not. The church has not embraced "marriage equality." Neither ecclesiastical law nor the prayer book entitles two persons to marry each other, or a member of the clergy to officiate at the marriage, unless one of the two is a woman and the other a man. General Convention did nothing to change that. The rite it did approve studiously avoids the terminology of marriage, let alone matrimony. What the presider pronounces when all is said and done is that the couple are "bound to one another in a holy covenant, as long as they both shall live." Whether this form of words can be construed as constituting *civil* marriage in those states that permit two women or two men to marry, the lawyers will have to decide. If they decide it can, the paradoxical consequence would seem to be that a same-sex couple, legally married by an Episcopal cleric acting with episcopal permission as an agent of the state, will *not* be married according to the church's own rubrics and canons.

Appearances notwithstanding, then, the new liturgy makes no claim that couples of the same sex can, in the ecclesiastical sense, marry. What it does say is more interesting. It says, explicitly and by implication, that two persons, both men or both women, are capable of making with each other a covenant so sacred, so religiously or spiritually significant, as to invite public recognition, welcome, celebration, and benediction on the part of a Christian community in an act of Christian worship. Since this capability is not, perhaps, self-evident, it needs to be argued for, and the argument needs to refute a well-worn syllogism: "The church can bestow its blessing only on what God already favors. But God does not favor same-sex coupling; far from it. Therefore . . ."

The commission that framed the new rite appears to have taken this reasoning seriously, though without drawing the same conclusion. The long apologia they provided for bishops and deputies at Convention implicitly accepts the major premise: liturgical blessing is not creation *ex nihilo*. It does make something new begin to happen, but does so on the basis of something that, by the grace of God, is already happening. A formal blessing on the part of the church is at once a thanksgiving for what happens and a petition for its continuation, enhancement, perfection. It follows that *promises*, effectual "speech-acts" that initiate but do not necessitate some determinate future, are eminently blessable—depending, however, on *what* future is being promised. In the case of the new liturgy, two persons promise to support and care, hold and cherish, honor and love, forsaking all others, as long as they both shall live—vows much the same as those made by brides and bridegrooms. The theological question is not whether two women or two men can genuinely utter this kind of performative speech. Of course they can. The question is what they are performing—what their speaking does, and whether doing it can be an effective sign, a "sacrament" of divine grace.

To judge by the rite itself and the apologia that comes with it, promising to live together faithfully and lovingly can be, God willing, cooperation with God in bringing about the eschatological consummation, the new creation, that is God's own promise. Or, to put it as the commission does, what this liturgy for witnessing and blessing witnesses and blesses is a covenant that embodies the church's "missional" character as the people of God in the world. Either way, it is collaborative participation in the divine purpose that makes the lifelong union of two persons not only blessable in itself but also a blessing to others.

By building its argument around the forward-looking, biblical notion of covenant, the commission responsible for proposing the new liturgy has taken a theological stand somewhat removed from the traditional Augustinian concern with quarantining sexuality. The vows themselves are traditional enough, but the rationale for blessing them has shifted towards discerning in relations of intimacy anticipations of the life of the world to come. This shift— from Genesis to Revelation, so to say—is evident but not obtrusive throughout the new liturgy. It appears in the opening address to the congregation, in the collects and the petitions of the litany, and (if they are used) in the eucharistic preface and postcommunion prayer. At no point, however, does the wording call attention to the fact that the two principal ministers of this sacramental action are both men or both women. Opening a space for that fact was the reason for composing a new liturgy in the first place, yet it is almost incidental to the liturgy as composed. The authorized text could be used, just as it stands, by a man and a woman. Were they to use it, they would be inaugurating a covenant with the same content, meaning, and purpose as the one same-sex couples will make. Conversely, it would seem that the theological rationale for blessing a same-sex couple's union applies equally well to marriage as the Episcopal Church now defines it.

Liturgies, however, are by nature polyvalent. They can be understood and used variously. Not every bishop is likely to allow even "provisional" use of the new text, and those who do allow it will no doubt take different positions on exactly what is allowed. In one diocese, at the moment, same-sex couples must sign a formal declaration of their understanding that the rite of blessing confers no status of any kind under civil law, and that whatever spiritual value it may have, it is not matrimony. The rite they are permitted to use is itself pared down to a litany followed by the blessing, which must be inserted between the Creed and the Passing of the Peace at the Eucharist appointed for the day. Neither an exchange of vows nor proper prayers and lessons are included. By contrast with this minimalist implementation of General Convention's enactment, one diocese in a state where same-sex couples may enter into civil marriage has gone a step further in the direction that the rite itself seems to suggest. Diocesan clergy have their bishop's permission to use a single rite when presiding at a marriage—any marriage. The rite they are to use is again a modification of the one that Convention approved, but instead of emphasizing a difference between same-sex and mixed-sex unions, the changes, which are small and few, imply that there *is* no difference.

The official exposition of the new rite's theology, although it does not demand this more expansive interpretation, is certainly open to it. The point of the argument is not to justify covenants between persons of the same sex on grounds that are unique or special or exceptional. Rather, the commission's approach has evidently been to regard these promises and the promises made at conventional weddings in the same light, as variations on a single theme. Accordingly, it might be argued that the new rite is "provisional" in more senses than one. Not only is it a tentative, preliminary experiment, subject to replacement by something better, like the trial-use services of the 1970s. More importantly, it may turn out to be a temporary measure, which serves a purpose for the time being but for which, some day, there may be no need. That would be the case if the church should find itself realizing that the bond and covenant of marriage is one, in every sense that matters, whether it unites two husbands, two wives, or one of each. If that is so, why have "separate but equal" liturgies at all?

❖ ❖ ❖

Charles Hefling is the academic editor of The Oxford Guide to the Book of Common Prayer. *He has served as editor-in-chief of the* Anglican Theological Review *and taught systematic theology for thirty years as a professor at Boston College.*

"The Celebration and Blessing of a Marriage," The Book of Common Prayer (1979)	"The Witnessing and Blessing of a Lifelong Covenant" authorized for provisional use 2012

The Collect
O gracious and everliving God,
you have created us male and female
   in your image:
Look mercifully upon this man and
   this woman who come to you
   seeking your blessing,
and assist them with your grace,
that with true fidelity and steadfast
   love they may honor and keep the
   promises and vows they make;
   through Jesus Christ our Savior,
who lives and reigns with you in the
   unity of the Holy Spirit, one God,
   for ever and ever.
	The Collect
	Gracious and everliving God:
	assist by your grace *N.* and *N.*,
	whose lifelong commitment of love
	   and fidelity we witness this day.
	Grant them your blessing, that with
	   firm resolve
	they may honor and keep the cov-
	   enant they make;
	through Jesus Christ our Savior,
	who lives and reigns with you in the
	   unity of the Holy Spirit, one God,
	   for ever and ever.

The Marriage
In the Name of God,
I, *N.*, take you, *N.*, to be my wife
   (husband),
to have and to hold from this
   day forward,
for better for worse,
for richer for poorer,
in sickness and in health,
to love and to cherish,
until we are parted by death.
This is my solemn vow.
	The Commitment
	In the name of God,
	I, *N.*, give myself to you, *N.*
	I will support and care for you:
	enduring all things, bearing
	   all things.
	I will hold and cherish you:
	in times of plenty, in times of want.
	I will honor and love you:
	forsaking all others, as long as we
	   both shall live.
	This is my solemn vow.

Continued

"The Celebration and Blessing of a Marriage *Continued*	"The Witnessing and Blessing of a Lifelong Covenant" *Continued*

The Blessing of the Marriage
 God the Father, God the Son,
 God the Holy Spirit,
 bless, preserve, and keep you;
 the Lord mercifully with his favor
    look upon you, and fill you with all
    spiritual benediction and grace;
 that you may faithfully live together
    in this life, and in the age to come
    have life everlasting.
	The Blessing of the Couple
	 God the Father, God the Son,
	 God the Holy Spirit,
	 bless, preserve, and keep you,
	 and mercifully grant you rich and
	    boundless grace,
	 that you may please God in body
	    and soul.
	 God make you a sign of the loving-
	    kindness
	 and steadfast fidelity manifest in the
	    life, death,
	 and resurrection of our Savior,
	 and bring you at last to the delight
	    of the heavenly banquet,
	 where he lives and reigns for ever
	    and ever.

CHAPTER 12

Queen Bubba Finds a Home

Thomas Dukes

In the fall of 1993, a friend suggested that I try Church of Our Saviour, Episcopal, in Akron, Ohio; he knew I'd been church shopping for years with no luck. Raised Southern Baptist and with a short but unfortunate sojourn into Catholicism behind me, I wanted the acceptance of a radical church, the formalism of a traditional one. I did not have what it takes to be a Unitarian or an atheist. Although my friend's partner and he had tried Church of Our Saviour and found it too high, he thought I might like it. He was wrong.

Turned out, I loved it. And it loved me right back.

Based on my Southern Baptist upbringing, I knew that a) all Episcopalians were millionaires, and b) they could drink without guilt. Thus, I wore my best suit, purchased at the short-lived Cleveland branch of Barney's of New York; the suit was Donna Karan, but everyone thought it was Armani. I believed this would be a one-time visit; no way would I fit in at an Episcopal church. I was not a millionaire, I could not drink without guilt, and I was, in the parlance of an earlier day, queer as a three-dollar bill.

I tried not to arrive too early, so I would not be sitting in a pew alone for too long. On the other hand, I did not want to make a late entrance and be stared at. It is a truth not universally acknowledged that few things are more difficult than a single person going to a new church for the first time alone, especially if that person is gay.

I was a little too early for my plan to work; after I slid into a pew, halfway down the center aisle and, I felt, a non-committal choice, two or three strangers made it a point to introduce themselves most cordially. Just before the service began, the priest, in more robes than I'd ever seen on a cleric, greeted me very warmly. Nonetheless, I had no real plans to return, especially after trying to navigate the confusing Book of Common Prayer.

I might not have returned, either, except that at the end of the service, the church's director of Christian education grabbed me by the arm with a force that would have impressed my Army sergeant father and pulled me—I mean, escorted me—to the Room with the Big Blue Rug where coffee hour was held. Here, while being fussed over and welcomed, I processed my observations:

1. The gay people here were not hiding, they were not discreet, they were not careful. Nor were they making a point to show off their gayness unless they wanted to. They just *were*.

2. At most, four or five people were rich. Everyone else was like me—middle-class professional—or working-class or downright poor.

3. Most of the people were straight. With kids. Whom they wanted to be around gay people and people of color and old people and people who came off the street needing something and . . . everybody else.

4. People were doing their very best to live the gospel.

5. The priest was gay.

And so I found my church home.

❖ ❖ ❖

Over the next eighteen years, I would become a full-fledged church queen, which isn't the point. The point is that the people at church, straight, gay, and God-knows-what, *wanted* me to become a full-fledged church queen. I was not tolerated; I was not admitted so the church could make a point about its inclusivity and diversity. I was *welcomed*.

Off and on during those next years, I polished altar brass; served on the vestry for two-and-a-half terms as its clerk (and caught hell from the diocese over my disrespectful minutes); taught Sunday school to teenagers with two different co-teachers; sang (well, sorta) in the choir; became the second man to become part of the coffee hour hospitality team, eventually coordinating it; became a Sunday morning lector and usher; worked rummage sales; administered communion to the home-bound for a brief period; served as chalice bearer on Sunday mornings once a month or so; became a reliable substitute when others did not show.

In doing these ministries, I became, without realizing it all, a part of the church community. I was confirmed in the Episcopal Church about four years after I began attending, but that was almost irrelevant. Church of Our Saviour, in my view, was a genuine church family but more than that, it was a true church community. Gay people—and more came after I did to join those of us who were already there—flourished because we were welcomed, but we were only one group that was welcomed. The priest and the vestry wanted, truly, for everyone to come, street folks and rich folks whose families had been there for generations, and everyone in between. For many folks, attendance at church required a lot of healing from horrendous experiences with religion as they grew up; for others, the idea of worship of any kind was very new. LGBT or not, folks came and went as they needed; Church of Our Saviour was always there (and may it always be there), a wonderful touchstone living the Gospels by service to the poor in the community and to its members, by celebration of the Father, Son, and Holy Spirit on Sundays and other services.

I wish I could say all of this came without cost. It did not.

✜ ✜ ✜

I met my partner in 1998; we moved in together at the end of 1999 and were joined in civil union in Vermont in 2000, then married in Canada in 2002. I had just assumed our union could at least be blessed in the church, but I assumed incorrectly. Our priest would have performed such a ceremony in our home but not in church or anywhere else. In fairness—and that priest was and is a wonderful man—I must note that the Episcopal Church had not even officially considered same-sex blessings at this point. Having been raised a Southern Baptist, I was used to churches with a great deal of autonomy and did not fully understand why the priest could not go his own way. Given that he himself was gay (something that remained a hard pill to swallow for some of the old-timers), the priest might well have put his job at risk had he blessed our civil union and, later, marriage.

Still, his declining to bless our union in church stung; it stung even more when his successor performed such a blessing five days after she arrived. (The preliminary work with the couple had been done before she began her duties.)

Although he joined the church, I don't think my partner felt much of an emotional or spiritual investment in church after we were denied the opportunity to have our marriage blessed there. I loved the church so much that I swallowed hard and took it on the chin. Nonetheless, this marked the beginning of my realizing that the church I loved so much sometimes talked one talk but walked a different one. That this was inevitable was something I understood intellectually but not emotionally; going to the back of the bus has not been my style since I left home.

In the meantime, however, Church of Our Saviour offered many joys. I made friends who are friends to this day, and I hope always will be. More than that, I *belonged*. I knew that I belonged when Betty Yoe chewed me out for being the first cookie person to openly bring store-bought cookies to coffee hour; immediately afterwards, we became great pals, and I saw her a few days before she died in a local nursing home. I knew I belonged when a preoperative transsexual could come Sundays on her one day off for as long as she needed, simply to be. After my mother passed away and I brought my piano home, it sat loved but ignored in my sun room until one of our choir members, a public school music teacher, heard that I wanted to find it a good home; she took it for her children, and the beloved instrument found new life. *I had something—more than one thing—to give*. When I wound up in the hospital, the church's florist sent me flowers; I got calls from fellow parishioners, most of whom saw me only on Sundays.

I went every Sunday that I was in town and not sick; I finally found my seat in the back row where I could pitch in at the last minute as a substitute usher or what-have-you. I was there for the Easters when we ran out of chairs; I was there for the Easters when you could more or less have set off a bomb and inconvenienced no one. I was there when an interim gave a sermon to something like thirty people on a Sunday morning (thirty unhappy people, I regret to say). I was there at funerals for the elderly who had welcomed me into the church that was changing as the world changed; I was there for baptisms of infants and adults.

All of this sounds like the life of a typical church, and it was, but the increasing gay membership inevitably rocked the boat. The middle years of my membership at Church of Our Saviour were glorious for others and for me, but not all were happy. As the attendance of gays grew with the resulting membership increase of same, the balance of power shifted. Gay men and lesbians began cropping up in significant roles on committees and on the vestry; many of these folks were well-educated, had professional jobs, and were used to being heard. Having been invited to the party, we intended to participate. The underlying tension was, I guess, inevitable, and several attempts were made to bring it out in the open, all of them circumvented one way or the other.

Several factors prevented an open dialogue. First, several of the church leaders were conflict avoidant, believing—and they may well have been correct—that there was little to say that we didn't already know. Still, by never having a vestry meeting or parish-wide conversation on the subject, neither side got to have its say and clear the air. Second, a good bit of the problem may have been simply generational. Finally, the priest himself, for reasons of his own, could not encourage or facilitate such a conversation. Most sadly and ironically, the new openness, inclusivity, and diversity led to some of the long-time members feeling that they were no longer welcome in their own church. Citing other reasons for going, they left.

Granted, some of those leavings were the natural stuff of life: job transfers, retirement moves, etc. Yet, that we lost some members—members of long standing—due to the emerging gay presence at church simply cannot be denied. I didn't know what to do with that knowledge then, and I don't know now. I do know that everyone who left remained very cordial with me, which makes me think their leaving perhaps had less to do with the whole gay thing than some people think. I do believe the small church began to have an undeniable in-group, and some members of long standing felt left out. For others, the church seemed to be moving away from them and no longer felt like their church home even as it became a church home to others of us.

I never dreamed that I would leave someday, too.

But I did.

❖ ❖ ❖

For reasons completely unrelated to my place as a gay member of the congregation, I left Church of Our Saviour this past year. I now attend the large Episcopal church three miles from my former parish. Its rector has been nothing less than cordial and warm to me. The other members are as friendly as I will allow. I go each Sunday for the sermon, communion, a cup of coffee and a cookie. Then I go home. Everyone is perfectly nice, but it is not home and perhaps will never be.

Nonetheless, I have taken the best of Church of Our Saviour with me in memories of Christmases and Easters and Holy Weeks and the memorial service for a family-less man who had died of

AIDS and been baptized on his death bed. A dozen or so of us showed up at noon for the memorial of someone we had never met but who was a child of God and deserved to be remembered. The rector's words were brief but some of his best.

I left my spouse after eleven years of marriage on January 2, 2011, and the rector showed up to help me with a few boxes but stayed all day and made endless trips back and forth to my new home, a rental from a church friend who had come to my rescue, lowering the rent on her former home by hundreds so I could afford to stay there. I cannot remember what the rector said, but she made me see, feel, absorb, and understand something that has sustained me ever since: Even the end of a marriage that had begun so well was holy work that had to be done for both my spouse's and my sakes.

Wherever I go, whatever I do, Church of Our Saviour will be my church home. I love it with the completeness of a first, great love; I love it in spite of its few flaws and because of its many virtues.

May it please God that in the days of declining memberships and closing churches, Church of Our Saviour lasts forever. It will in my heart.

❖ ❖ ❖

Thomas Dukes lives and writes in Akron, OH. He is the author of Baptist Confidential, *a prize-winning poetry collection; a memoir,* Sugar Blood Jesus; *and other works of poetry, fiction, non-fiction, and scholarship. Born in central Florida, he grew up in western South Carolina. He received his BA and MA from The University of Texas at El Paso and his doctorate from Purdue University.*

CHAPTER 13

Will You Respect the Dignity of Every Human Being?

A Latino Perspective on Same-Sex Blessing

Daniel Vélez-Rivera

Latino immigrants are on a journey of transformation as we shed some of the old ways and learn to accept new ways of thinking, being, and living. The Pacto Bautismal (Baptismal Covenant) and the Holy Bible define for Episcopal Christians how we should live our lives: with dignity, while upholding the dignity of all others. Given what the gospels tell us about Jesus including the marginalized, why should I do otherwise?

Somewhere along my faith journey to ordination, I learned to respect marginalized people. So when I'm asked why I would bless same-sex couples, or invite lesbian, gay, bisexual, transgendered, or questioning (LGBTQ) people to the eucharistic table, or why anyone should support and affirm their LGBTQ daughter, son, grandchild, nephew, goddaughter, or neighbor, I have two responses. The first is that we are made in God's image and are to respect the dignity of others. The other is that God doesn't make mistakes.

At baptisms, Easter, and other special occasions of the church, Spanish- and English-speaking Episcopalians turn to *El Libro de Oración Común* (pp. 224–5) or the Book of Common Prayer (pp. 304–5) to reaffirm their baptismal covenant, which is based on the Apostles' Creed. The congregation also responds to five questions affirming that, with God's help, we hope to live into faithful lives and to uphold just Christian values. The fifth question of the covenantal inquiry is:

"¿Lucharás por la justicia y la paz entre todos los pueblos, y respetarás la dignidad de todo ser humano?"

"Will you strive for justice and peace among all people, and respect the dignity of every human being?"

Lucharás (to strive) is a hopeful verb that allows us to live into the possibility of oneness that Christ wants for us. We respond, "Así lo haré, con el auxilio de Dios," "I will, with God's help," to commit to this promise. Fully affirming these words with heart and mind is easier said than done, particularly when one's humanness, context, culture, and personal values clash with a theology that underscores justice for all, goodness by all, and the Divine in all of God's creation.

How do Latinos/as overcome the pain, the shame, the fear, or the feelings of disgrace that can be associated with being, being related to, or even associating with LGBTQ people? It can be especially difficult when coming from a culture that is stereotypically *machista* and oftentimes defined by conservative Christian values. How do Latinos/as accept their child, grandchild, brother, mother, sister, father, nephew, goddaughter, or neighbor as LGBTQ?

I have had the opportunity to initiate open and respectful conversations addressing the taboo subject of human sexual identity with Latino parishioners of several generations, in hopes of making this topic less taboo. Through these dialogues I strive to fulfill my own baptismal covenant by invoking God and using scripture to open the hearts and minds of those who might not understand or accept how God sustains and blesses God's homosexual, bisexual, and transgendered creation. In this dialectical journey with members of my faith community, it is a privilege to invite them, in a safe and respectful conversation, to share their emotions and understanding of God's purpose regarding the sacredness of all people made in the image of God. It is possible for Latino immigrants in the United States to understand how marginalization and exclusion toward Latinos/as parallels the exclusion of LGBTQ people in the church and society. Latino immigrants experience fear, identity challenges, exclusion, and subtle or overt prejudices in similar ways to their LGBTQ counterparts in this country.

These difficult conversations are best held in small groups. One way in which I try to guide women, men, and youth into a transformational experience of inclusivity and unconditional acceptance has been through Bible studies and small-group meetings that focus on moral reasoning. In my experience, people are more likely to share even their most profound sentiments, ideologies, feelings, and divine understanding of God's purpose for humanity in intimate settings. I have learned that the new generation Latino/a (fourteen to thirty-four years old) in the United States does not seem to have the same traditional values or beliefs around human sexuality as their elders and are somehow better able to understand differences. I have found it particularly transformative in gatherings where children, youth, and young adults address their questions of faith around diverse sexual identities.

In October 2012, the Pew Forum on Religion and Public Life published results of a national political survey in "Latinos, Religion and Campaign 2012." The study presented how Latinos/as of diverse political affiliations would likely vote in the 2012 presidential election. The questions included Latino opinions regarding legal rights for gays and lesbians to marry,[1] a question that crosses into socio-religious, moral, ethical, and cultural values. The Pew Forum used the term "homosexual" in addressing this demographic, as does the Episcopal Church when it refers to same-sex couples seeking the blessing of their union.

The survey revealed that "for the first time since the Pew Hispanic Center began asking the question in its National Survey of Latinos, more Hispanics favored allowing gays and lesbians to marry legally (52%) than opposed same-sex marriage (34%)." This survey indicated that the Latino response to same-sex marriage was in accordance with the general public and also with the Pew Hispanic Center's 2011 National Survey of Latinos,[2] in which 59 percent of Hispanics said that homosexuality should be accepted by society, while 30 percent said it should be discouraged by society.

The trend among diverse ethnic Latinos/as who are eligible to vote in the United States regarding the rights of homosexuals to marry is changing. Is the sociological trend toward homosexuals manifested in the pews of our Latino Episcopal churches changing

---

1. The Pew Forum on Religion and Public Life, October 18, 2012, *http://www.pewforum. org/Race/Latinos-Religion-and-Campaign-2012.aspx#gay*

2. Pew Research Center, *http://www.pewhispanic.org/2012/04/04/appendix-a-2011-national-survey-of-latinos-survey-methodology/*

as well? I would say yes, and as the Pew poll indicated, more and more people are accepting. At least 10 percent or more of the members in the congregation I now serve are LGBTQ, partly because I am gay, but also because the Christian moral and ethical values that I espouse around inclusivity and diversity in the church affirm and respect the dignity of *all* people. The Pew Hispanic Center's statistics are personally reassuring and support my ministry to *all* people, especially the new generation Latino community that is opening itself to transformation in ways that integrate their ancestral values with their new cultural vision as immigrants in this country.

Blessing others, which I believe is a manner of loving others regardless of our opinions and personal human restrictions, is both arduous and complex. Even as we want to accept God's will, we are challenged by our human free will. Humanity has always been told what is wrong, sinful, and unacceptable, and LGBTQ people have long fallen into categories of wrongness in the socio-cultural makeup of our communities, regardless of culture or ethnicity. So, does God make mistakes? Is that what LGBTQ people are? It is possible to *luchar* (strive) to act as Christ acted when one also affirms that with God all things are possible (Mark 10:27). Scripture gives us a Great Commandment: "Amar al prójimo como a sí mismo," "Love one's neighbor as oneself" (Matthew 22:35–40, Mark 12:28–34, and Luke 10:25–28). The miracle of God's divine action was revealed in my congregation when most people in the parish embraced a gay teen, a transgendered young adult, gay and lesbian parishioners, my spouse, and me—their gay priest.

Shifting from a political survey like the Pew study to the reality in the pews of an Episcopal Latino congregation is where the Baptismal Covenant gets tested. ¿Lucharás por la justicia y la paz entre todos los pueblos, y respetarás la dignidad de todo ser humano? When asked by my Latino parishioners whether LGBTQ people are sinners and condemned to hell, I remind them that Jesus covenanted with humanity to follow in his footsteps so that they would receive the promise of eternal life (salvation). Why do we Latinos, or people of any ethnicity, struggle with blessing same-sex couples when we affirm that all people are made in God's image, the same God whom we venerate and love?

Latino cultures, traditions, and values are as diverse as the colors of the rainbow. The range of responses by Latino Episcopalians to include and to bless LGBTQ people is likely no different than for people of any other ethnic group in the United States. The governing articles (polity) of the Episcopal Church in the United States give clergy and congregations the right to bless or not bless same-sex couples, and Latino Episcopalians have that same privilege.

I am astounded by the number of people who have no qualms about blessing animals during the feast of St. Francis of Assisi, yet are challenged to bless people. I believe that we should bless and affirm anyone who wishes to commit their love to one another before God and their faith community. Regardless of one's ethnicity, we may think that the blessing of same-sex couples is ungodly, unbiblical, un-Anglican, and unseemly, but what would Jesus do today if a same-sex couple wishing to be blessed reached out to touch the hem of his garment? The challenge we face in communities of faith is *luchar* (to strive) to bless and to love all of God's children, as called by Christ.

✤ ✤ ✤

The Reverend Daniel Vélez Rivera, ordained in 2006, planted an Episcopal Hispanic ministry in Salem, Massachusetts, and fostered the growth of this congregation into St. Peter's/San Pedro Episcopal Church—a bilingual, multicultural house of prayer for all people. He currently serves St. Gabriel's in Leesburg, Virginia, a monolingual English-language parish, and ten-year-old church plant. His pastoral, spiritual, evangelistic, and missional ministries revolve around representing Christ in the church and in the community. Daniel is married to Parker Gallagher, with whom he has shared seventeen years of life; they live in Reston, Virginia.

CHAPTER 14

Dearly Beloved[1]

Fredrica Harris Thompsett

This is an historic day. On this New Year's Day, ancient texts, modern rites, and post-modern justice are gaily aligned.

It seems fitting that Katherine and Mally have invited a person with impeccable historical and theological credentials to offer the homily! (Fortunately I am not a liturgist, as the happy couple could not agree on whether marriage is a "sacrament" or a "sacramental rite.") I do know that some of you may not have a good history with history. You may think it is mostly about memorizing odd dates and funny names. I think historical theology is mostly about putting collective memory to work in the service of justice.

So I invite us to put our collective memory to work by remembering the opening words of this service: "Dearly beloved." These words are addressed to each and every one of us. They come to us from one of our Anglican ancestors, and they are directed to the wider society, to the community gathered here today, *and* they are intended especially for Mally and Katherine.

---

1. This sermon was preached by Fredrica Harris Thompsett on January 1, 2011 at the celebration of the marriage of the Reverend Dr. Katherine Hancock Ragsdale and the Reverend Canon Mally Ewing Lloyd at the Cathedral Church of St. Paul, Boston, Massachusetts.

Anglicans were among the first early modern Christians to put a loving spin on marriage. Thomas Cranmer, author of the earliest English Book of Common Prayer, crafted a liturgy which underscored marriage as a positive opportunity for mutual enjoyment.[2] Cranmer—himself a happily, if quietly, married man with children—emphasized the benefit of marriage for England's citizens. Marriage was, he said, for the "mutual society, help and comfort that the one ought to have of the other, both in prosperity and adversity." Perhaps with his own "dearly beloved Margaret Cranmer" in mind, Cranmer added to an official marriage text for the first time promises that each partner would "love and cherish" the other! These words replaced the wife's required oath in the late medieval service to be "buxom in bed and board."

What I do want to emphasize is that today's service might aptly and historically be described as "traditionally Anglican." Archbishop Cranmer recognized marriage as a "vital social institution" grounded in ideals of mutuality, help, and comfort. Similarly we are reminded by today's reading from "Goodridge vs. Department of Health" that church and society must never hoard these values or take their wider beneficial intent for granted.[3]

There are, as well, theological lessons and echoes to be savored in the phrase "dearly beloved." In today's service we, the people of God, are greeted with words saturated in hospitality. Think of it: Each one of us is welcomed from the start as "beloved." Such language

---

2. Diarmaid MacCulloch, *Thomas Cranmer: A Life* (New Haven, CT: Yale University Press, 1996), pp. 420–21.

3. The landmark ruling in "Goodridge vs. the Department of Health," the State Appellate Court presided over by Chief Justice Margaret Marshall, resulted in Massachusetts becoming the first U.S. state to issue marriage licenses to same-sex couples. This action was decided in November of 2003 and became law in May of 2004. It has withstood attempts to replace the word "marriage" with second-class images like "civil union."

has enormous implications for how we view ourselves, our bodies, and our society. Who is beloved? More pointedly: Who is worthy of being "beloved?" Theology is, after all, about ethics.

But wait: Where have we heard that word "beloved" before? Is this not the same word God proclaims in the synoptic Gospels' telling of our Lord's Baptism: in the acclamation of God's own "well-beloved Son." In baptism we too are acclaimed "beloved ones" and enrolled "as Christ's own forever."

What the heck, those of you who know me know I see traces and echoes of lifelong baptismal vitality. Here's just one more enticing possibility. Could it be that Chief Justice Margaret Marshall, herself an Anglican, was influenced by the promises in the Baptismal Covenant to "respect the dignity of every human being"? Did not Marshall, writing for the majority in the "Goodridge" case, argue for "affirm[ing] the dignity and equality of all individuals"? Could it be that common prayer actually has a steadily progressive impact influencing both individual hearts *and* societal laws?

Most of all, could it be that in the midst of today's celebration we are once again learning to look with God's eyes? Could it be that we are learning again and again to recognize that every child is conceived in the image of God? Could it be that the presence of God in all living things—in "all creatures of our God and King"—is what makes them beautiful? Could it be that in this celebration and blessing of a marriage we are doing our best to model, to teach society by our example to look with God's eyes, proclaiming no one, no community, no part of God's beloved creation is ugly or unclean?[4]

---

4. J. Philip Newell, *Listening for the Heartbeat of God: A Celtic Spirituality* (New York: Paulist Press, 1997); see pp. 11–13 for his interpretation of Pelagius's wisdom.

This bold and godly teaching takes serious and committed leadership. I invite you to join me in giving a "shout out" to the Diocese of Massachusetts—to all lay and clergy leaders—and especially on this bright New Year's Day to Bishop Tom Shaw![5]

Katherine and Mally, I have not forgotten you. You are and have been held deeply in my heart. I rejoice in your courage, your several commitments, your public and pastoral witness, and most of all your delight in naming one another as "dearly beloved."

The Goodridge reading describes the decision to marry as one of "life's *momentous* acts of self-definition." The two of you apparently made this momentous decision at the same time and we rejoice in it. On this historic day in your lives we are honored to witness and uphold your loving promises.

Yet Mally and Katherine, my "dearly beloved" friends, I wonder what images, what words, what memories will carry you forward in the days and nights ahead?

Will your love, like that of Ruth, be determined, steadfast, loyal, and most of all marked by "ready availability"?[6] This availability thing is a big challenge, a momentous challenge, perhaps particularly for those of us with pastoral hearts and pastoral responsibilities. Will your love be reminiscent of the *hesed*—the steadfast loving-kindness of God?

Will your love, in shared tribute to Mary and Martha, welcome the wholeness of longing for and laboring for the reign of God?

---

5. In November of 2009, Episcopal Bishop M. Thomas Shaw—following a permissive (though not obligatory) action of General Convention—permitted clergy in this diocese to officiate at same-sex weddings. This is the first such celebration in which Bishop Shaw presided and signed the marriage license.

6. I owe the phrase "ready availability" to Joan Chittister, *The Friendship of Women: The Hidden Tradition of the Bible* (New York: BlueBridge, 2006), pp. 60–61.

Talk about a huge challenge—who would have the time, let alone the energy to do it all?

The truly Good News, my two "dearly beloved friends," is that God in Christ has already acted for us! It is only by being grounded in God's love that we are able to see the image of God in one another morning by morning and day by day, that we are able to call one another "dearly beloved" at morn and at close of day.

Dearly beloved, one and all, on this truly historic day, let the word go forth that we are invited to love ourselves and one another the way God loves us. It is both that simple and it is that profound.

✠ ✠ ✠

Dr. Fredrica Harris Thompsett is Mary Wolfe Professor Emerita of Historical Theology at Episcopal Divinity School in Cambridge, Massachusetts. She is the author of several books on Episcopal history, Anglican theology, and baptismal ministry.